D1738188

NEIGHBORHOOD JUSTICE IN CAPITALIST SOCIETY

Recent Titles in
Contributions in Political Science
Series Editor: Bernard K. Johnpoll

NEIGHBORHOOD JUSTICE IN CAPITALIST SOCIETY

The Expansion of the Informal State

RICHARD HOFRICHTER

Contributions in Political Science, Number 171

GREENWOOD PRESS

New York · Westport, Connecticut · London

Library of Congress Cataloging-in-Publication Data

Hofrichter, Richard.
  Neighborhood justice in capitalist society.

  (Contributions in political science,
ISSN 0147-1066 ; no. 171)
  Bibliography: p.
  Includes index.
  1. Neighborhood justice centers—United States.
  2. Dispute resolution (Law)—United States.
  3. Sociological jurisprudence.   4. Capitalism—United
States. I. Title. II. Series.
  KF9084.H65   1987   347.73   86-33654
                              347.307

  ISBN 0-313-25677-2 (lib. bdg. : alk. paper)

Library of Congress Catalog Card Number: 86-33654
ISBN: 0-313-25677-2
ISSN: 0147-1066

First published in 1987

Greenwood Press, Inc.
88 Post Road West, Westport, Connecticut 06881

Printed in the United States of America

The paper used in this book complies with the
Permanent Paper Standard issued by the National
Information Standards Organization (Z39.48-1984).

10 9 8 7 6 5 4 3 2 1

Copyright Acknowledgments

To the memory of Bernard Kutner

Contents

Acknowledgments

Every work involves the contributions and support of many people. My greatest intellectual and personal debt is to Mike Brown, mentor and friend over the last decade, who encouraged me to write this book, provided substantial insights, and read many versions. During these same years, Robert Engler's encouragement and advice as teacher and friend have been invaluable. Gratitude is owed as well to those who read and commented on portions of the manuscript, including Paul Stern, Sue Stern, Peter Wengert, Marilyn Richter, Deborah Baskin, and Stanley Aronowitz. A special thanks to Christine Harrington for eight years of discussions and helpful suggestions about neighborhood dispute resolution. I would also like to acknowledge those who played no active role in the preparation of the book but nonetheless influenced some of what was finally produced. They include Richard Abel, Richard Quinney, Laura Nader, Sally Merry, Susan Silbey, Boa Santos, Craig McEwen, Leonard Buckle, and Suzann Thomas-Buckle. Many thanks to the staffs of the neighborhood dispute resolution programs who allowed me to interview them and gave generously of their time and knowledge. A special thanks to Lawrence Freedman and Larry Ray of the Special Committee on Dispute Resolution of the American Bar Association and to Madeleine Crohn of the National Institute for Dispute Resolution for their cooperation. Thanks to Diane Goldman who performed acts of wizardry on the word processor. My survival during the writing of this book was due, in no small measure, to the consistent support and friendship of Joan Rodman and Janice Ball. Finally, thanks to Mim Vasan and Lisa Reichbach at Greenwood Press for their assistance with all aspects of publishing this book.

Introduction

The management of interpersonal social conflict in everyday life within the American judicial system is changing. Of particular import is the reemergence of informal, decentralized alternatives to courts for the resolution of a wide range of citizen disputes and grievances, both civil and criminal (see Ray et al., 1986; Goldberg et al., 1985; Marks et al., 1984; McGillis, 1982). Neighborhood dispute resolution (NDR), one manifestation of this trend, is offered as a possible solution to the inaccessibility and expense of courts and a way to resolve conflict in a voluntary, peaceable manner, without lawyers. Proponents argue that NDR is more appropriate, equitable, final, efficient, speedier, and fairer than adjudication. However, NDR is not what it seems to be, but rather an alien institution inserting itself into the community, using the discourses, interactions, and values of community culture against itself.

More than an alternative to courts, NDR represents an alternative to politics and community organizing which lacks any organic connection to communities. It is an institution of social crisis management rather than justice. And what it manages is conflict and consciousness with a new profession of mediators. At a time of economic dislocation, the failure of traditional institutions of social integration, and a need to legitimate austerity, NDR is a highly seductive arrangement. At the same time, its pretense of self-empowerment and the suggestion that conflict need not be handled through the rule of law offers a possibility for challenge to state authority. Why does NDR arise again now? Who owns it?

The central thesis of this book is that the latest phase of mostly government-sponsored neighborhood dispute resolution forums that handle interpersonal disputes are primarily institutions of state social and political control (rather than dispute resolution). My proposition is that NDR falsely affirms the neighborhood as the basis of justice in the community through a discourse and process that reifies community—it presents an idea of community and collective self-help that is contrived, uses community culture against itself as a form of regulation and, by its presence, distracts attention from broader community issues. The practices of NDR paradoxically help to constitute the order of capitalism as much as undermine it. They emerge indirectly from class conflict between capital and labor as played out in communities. NDR centers derive from the consequence of social crisis in capital accumulation, the extraction of labor, and the capitalist state. These crises concern political and ideological struggles. They are also the result of resistance by citizens to the management of everyday social life by an expanded network of state agencies. They represent a major change in the form of the capitalist state and the reproduction of social relations. That form represents a shift toward what I will refer to as the informal state. The informal state is typified by an emphasis on cooperation and consensus, participation, and privatization. People are included by this institution rather than excluded as a means for drawing the individual more closely to the state, if not in allegiance than in the capacity to monitor and divert attention from issues outside its discourses. In this way, mediation is a form of self-policing. Moreover, the informal systems are forms of law, not isolated spheres. They remain connected to the formal legal system and legal concepts. Both are part of the state and rely on each other, even though the informal state creates an appearance of autonomy.

NDR is an instance of an emerging capitalist state in response to a new historical situation. Its significance lies in the way it operates through contradictory processes that confuse its meaning, defeat its declared purposes, and make its location within the state difficult to discern. The phenomenon is highly relevant for investigation as a major movement away from the rule of law and toward expanded state power. NDR, because it redefines conflict and changes how conflicts are handled, has important consequences for social justice, democracy, collective action, and social change. It is a thoroughly contradictory and unstable institution. The opportunity for social control coexists with a potential for self-empowerment and challenge. Ironically, it arose at a time of growing rights consciousness in the late 1960s and early 1970s—women's rights, environmental rights, children's rights, and, in general, person over property rights. This latest reemergence of NDR comes amid new social movements that cannot be contained by the formal legal system. At the same time, neighborhoods have been weakened by plant shutdowns, urban renewal, gentrification, and cutbacks in social services.

Most of the quasi-judicial and nonjudicial institutions and procedures referred to as alternatives to courts—informal justice,[1] mediation,[2] neighborhood dispute resolution (NDR), or neighborhood justice centers[3] have existed for many years. In the United States their roots can be traced to colonial times (Auerbach, 1983) and their modern forms to the mid-nineteenth century (Doo, 1973; Harrington, 1982).[4]

Contemporary models include conciliation, mediation, arbitration, ombudsmen, and administrative tribunals, to name but a few, and are used for disputes between individuals—such as family members, neighbors, landlords and tenants, merchants and consumers—and between groups or represented aggregates—such as management and labor and community organizations (see document I.1, a sample case). The procedures used are less formal and less adversarial than litigation. Mediation is also more particularistic, purposive, flexible, and less fact oriented. The structure and administration of programs vary, depending on the resources and objectives of project planners (Ray et al., 1986; Marks et al., 1984). There are also numerous nonprogrammatic processes, procedures, and activities that can be classified under the rubric of alternative dispute resolution. Proponents of mediation emphasize the mutually acceptable, voluntary nature of agreements between parties who know one another. They also argue that mediation is less coercive and costly than adjudication (Marks et al., 1984; Goldberg et al., 1985).

The development of informal, nonjudicial forums for dispute

Document 1.1
A Sample Case: A Neighbor's Barking Dogs

On Friday night, Mr. Merkle was awakened for the third time that night by the sound of barking dogs. A telephone call to his neighbor, Mr. Stearns, only resulted in a heated exchange, and the dogs continued to bark throughout the night. The next morning Merkle confronted Stearns about the dogs and about their phone conversation the night before. Tempers flared but this time Stearns assaulted Merkle. Mr. Merkle stormed off to call the Orange County Sheriff's Department, while Mr. Stearns put the dogs inside his house. When the deputy arrived, he saw no barking dogs. Because Merkle did not want to press assault charges, the deputy referred him to the Citizen Dispute Settlement Program.

Mr. Merkle decided to visit the program office where he explained his problem to the CDS staff. CDS then scheduled a hearing for the following Thursday night and sent Mr. Stearns a notice to come to the hearing. Both parties arrived at the local traffic court (where CDS hearings are held) that Thursday evening to attend the informal hearing. Mr. Trees, a local attorney who had volunteered to serve as their arbitrator, was introduced to them by the project director.

Trees:
Both of you gentlemen will have a chance to speak your piece so don't interrupt each other please. I'll have some questions and we'll try to get a clear view of the issue. Now, this is not a trial and I'm not a judge, we're trying to avoid that. What transpires here is not legally binding on anyone, so it doesn't prevent anyone from pursuing the traditional legal process. But, hopefully, you will take advantage of this opportunity. We'll try to reach some sort of a compromise agreement tonight.

Mr. Merkle started by stating that Mr. Stearns' dogs were keeping him awake at night. His bedroom window faced the yard where the dogs were kept. All he wanted, he said, was some peace and quiet at night.

Now it was Mr. Stearns' turn to tell his side of the story. He explained that he had gotten the dogs for protection because his house had been broken into several times. Mr. Stearns said that he had not heard the dogs barking. This only happened, he explained, when someone or something was in the yard. And, he added, no one is in the yard at night. Then the discussion started:

Merkle:
I hear them *very* clearly! You must be a heavy sleeper.

Why should *I* have to listen to your dogs?

Stearns:
I have the right to protect my home!

Trees:
OK, listen. Would you agree that Mr. Merkle has a right to enjoy his home and not be disturbed by dogs at unreasonable hours? And would you, Mr. Merkle, agree that Mr. Stearns has a right to have pets?

(Both nod in agreement)

Good, then let's start working toward a solution where you both can enjoy your rights and live next to each other in relative peace.

Within half an hour both parties agreed that Stearns would keep the dogs in the enclosed porch at night in an effort to reduce the barking. Both parties also agreed to stop threatening and yelling at each other. At the conclusion of the hearing, these agreements were written down and signed by both parties as a sign of good faith; each party received a copy of the agreement. Before they left, Merkle and Stearns separately rated their satisfaction with their hearing, and both stated they were quite satisfied.

About three weeks after the hearing, Merkle and Stearns were called by CDS and asked about the current situation with the dogs. Mr. Merkle replied that he was satisfied and that the dogs were quiet most nights. Mr. Stearns replied that he and Mr. Merkle did not speak much but that he had had no complaints or problems. Both parties were satisfied with the settlement they had reached at their hearing.

This sample case illustrates the procedures which are routinely used at CDS hearings. Following a hearing, both participants sign a statement listing the terms of the agreement, that is if they were able to reach one. Copies of this statement are given to both the complainant and respondent. The three-week follow-up illustrated in the example is not a standard practice; this occurs for a randomly-selected sample of complainants and respondents for evaluation purposes. But all clients make satisfaction ratings following their hearing, and these ratings constitute a separate part of the evaluation plan. If a respondent fails to appear for a hearing, the hearing is rescheduled. If a complainant fails to appear, the case is dropped.

resolution in the United States is neither linear nor uniform.
However, current experiments with informal justice, operating
under highly diverse conditions, differ from historical antecedents
in that the state now plays a greatly expanded role in planning
judicial institutions. Informal dispute resolution has been formalized on a national level. The scope, intensity, and pace of state
activity concerned with alternatives increased dramatically during
the mid-1970s, subsequent to urban riots and growing racial discord in the late 1960s (Aaronson, 1977; McGillis, 1982). The Law
Enforcement Assistance Administration (LEAA) funded numerous diverse "alternative" community justice pilot projects in the
early 1970s. Nationwide, over three hundred programs are operational today, many sponsored by local courts, local government,
business, bar associations, and criminal justice agencies.[5]

Although government-sponsored dispute resolution projects and
practices do not conform to a single organizational model, they
share some common characteristics. Most operate within the courts
or agencies connected with the courts, although some are independent. They normally accept cases referred by police, courts,
and prosecutors. A small proportion of cases come from social
service agencies or are "walk-ins." These may be more numerous
in programs located outside the courts. Cases referred by the
criminal justice system usually involve misdemeanors. Many dispute resolution programs also handle noncriminal disputes; some
even specialize in family, consumer, or landlord-tenant matters.
Once a case has been screened and accepted and the parties have
agreed to submit their dispute, an intake counselor or coordinator
contacts the parties, prepares them for the mediation session, and
collects background data. A hearing is then conducted before
trained, volunteer, usually nonlawyer mediators who reside in the
community or professional mediators with backgrounds in law,
psychology, or counseling. The dispute is usually resolved by some
form of third-party mediation or arbitration that produces an
agreement signed by each party. The dispositions may involve
referral of one or both parties to social services (see figures I.1 and
I.2 and document I.2 for a general depiction of the process common to some models). Noncompliance in criminal cases may result in return of the case to court for the resumption of the prosecution. The communities served by most programs tend to be

Figure 1.1
Citizen Dispute Settlement Process*

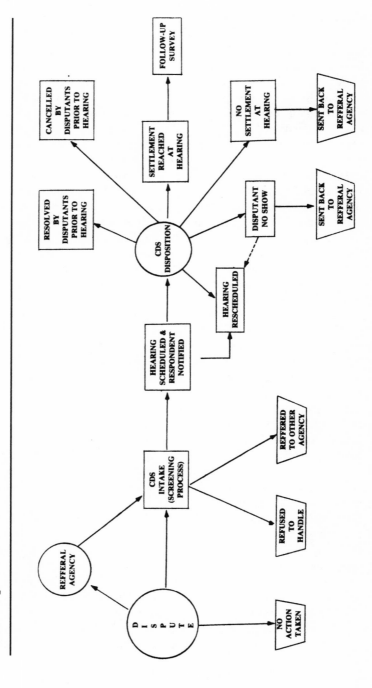

Figure 1.2
How Mediation Works

What steps are involved from the time a dispute is referred to a mediation program to the point when the situation is resolved? Below is an example:

Greg hired his 18-year-old neighbor, Paul, to mow the lawn and trim the hedges. When Greg returned to his house later that day, all the rosebushes had been cut in half. Furious that his plants had been ruined, he refused to pay Paul. When Paul demanded money for mowing the lawn, Greg hit him and warned him not to step on his property again. Paul went to court and applied for a complaint against Greg, charging him with Assault and Battery.

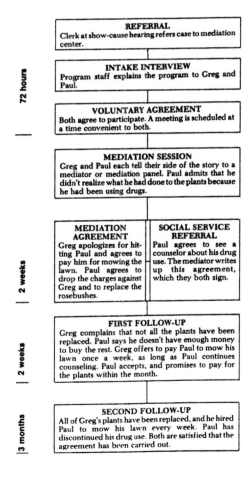

Document 1.2
Sample Program Brochure

Problem Solvers

Having an argument with your spouse, friend, landlord, neighbor, local merchant or employer?

Maybe the Neighborhood Justice Center can help you work out a quick, fair and lasting solution — at no cost to you!

The Center provides you with an alternative to the courts by offering a *free* mediation service.

How to Get the Center to Help Solve Your Problem.

1. If you think we can help you — call us at 523-8236, or come to the Center.

2. Our staff will listen to your problem and will advise you immediately if we can help you.

3. If we can help you, our staff will ask you for information concerning you, your problem and the person you have a complaint against.

4. We will then contact the other person and try to persuade him/her to agree to come to the Center to work out the problem with you and a neutral, trained mediator.

5. Next, we will schedule the case for mediation at a convenient time for both parties — during the day or evenings.

6. At the hearing, the mediator listens to both parties in an effort to learn how both would like to resolve the problem. The mediator does not decide who is right — he merely tries to get the parties to agree upon a solution.

7. When an agreement is reached, the specific things decided are written down by the mediator and signed by both parties.

Types of Disputes We Will Handle.

- **Domestic** problems involving family members

- **Neighborhood** problems — noise, pets, nuisances

- **Landlord-tenant** problems — security deposits, repairs, damages

- **Small claims** over money, personal property

- **Juvenile** problems — fights, vandalism

- **Consumer-merchant** problems — faulty merchandise, deposits, refunds, exchanges

- **Business Related** problems — employer/employee grievances

- **Educational** problems — involving handicapped students, administrative/staff/parent conflicts

lower middle class or poor, and disputants generally fall within lower income brackets and lack a college education (Sheppard et al., 1979; Delappa, 1983). Before elaborating on the thesis, we need to review significant recent historical developments in informal dispute resolution.

In 1976 the National Conference on the Causes of Popular Dissatisfaction with the Administration of Justice (the Pound Conference) was conducted in St. Paul, Minnesota and recommended "experimentation, evaluation, and widespread emulation of successful [dispute resolution] programs" (American Bar Association, 1976: 11). In 1978 the Office of Testing and Dissemination within LEAA provided funds for three eighteen-month experiments with neighborhood justice centers in Atlanta, Los Angeles, and Kansas City, sponsored by, respectively, a nonprofit agency with links to the courts, the local bar association, and the community services department of the city government, each operated in accordance with guidelines promulgated by LEAA (Lively, 1977). As LEAA terminated its contributions to these projects (which sought funding elsewhere) it continued to fund other projects. In 1980 the adjudication division established projects in Honolulu, Houston, and Washington, D.C. for another eighteen-month period. These programs are all located within the criminal justice system and are now referred to as Metropolitan Mediation Centers because their jurisdictions are citywide. The Office of Community Anti-Crime Programs, in conjunction with another federal agency supported ten additional experiments under the president's Urban Crime Prevention Program, many of which chose dispute settlement as one model of service (U.S. Department of Justice, LEAA/ACTION, 1980).

The Dispute Resolution Act of 1980 (PL 96-190) sought "to assist the States and other interested parties in providing to all persons convenient access to dispute resolution mechanisms which are effective, fair, inexpensive, and expeditious."[6] Although funds were never appropriated, many states enacted legislation on their own. In 1981 New York State became the first state to enact a law which appropriated funds ($1.1 million) for dispute resolution programs. Twenty other states had enacted comprehensive legislation or appropriated funds for mediation by 1986.[7] Many state and federal courts have established alternatives on their own as well.

Influential professional organizations, such as the American Bar Association, the National Center for State Courts, the Judicial Conference of the United States, the Conference of Chief Justices, the Society for Professionals in Dispute Resolution, and the American Arbitration Association, have advocated and encouraged informal procedures, as have newer organizations such as the National Peace Academy Campaign in Washington, D.C., established to develop support that would "teach, conduct and coordinate research in the methods of peacemaking, including conflict resolution" (Conner and Mapes, 1979). The former Chief Justice of the United States Supreme Court has given strong support to mediation and arbitration (Dispute Resolution, no. 8, 1982).

Major foundations were, for a time, active in the field, funding numerous projects. They included the Edna M. Clark, Rockefeller, Robert Wood Johnson, and Ford Foundations, the Lilly Endowment, and the Carnegie Corporation (Ford Foundation, 1978a). The Ford Foundation has produced a number of reports on the subject and, in 1979, awarded nearly $500,000 in grants to research or demonstration projects on alternative forms of resolving conflict (Ford Foundation, 1978a, 1978b). From 1973 to 1983 Ford spent almost $8 million for mediation experiments (Ford Foundation, 1983). More importantly, the Ford Foundation in conjunction with the Hewlett-Packard Foundation launched the National Institute for Dispute Resolution (NIDR) in 1983. With $1.5 million a year for five years, the Institute initiated some of the functions designated in the Dispute Resolution Act of 1980 which was not implemented. NIDR is a significant focal point, given its objectives to promote dispute settlement without litigation and its emphasis on the interests of policy makers. NIDR funds programs, conferences, teaching materials, and research in order to "put into practice satisfactory methods of settling disputes without resorting to courts [and] trials" (NIDR, 1984).

The Ford Foundation and Hewlett Foundation are still active in funding projects to promote the field's growth. The latter, along with NIDR, are deeply involved in providing grants to university centers (NIDR, 1986). The literature on NDR also proliferates. There are at least eight journals specializing in dispute resolution and dozens of books on the theory and practice of mediation (NIDR, 1986). The National Criminal Justice Reference Service contains a Dispute Resolution Center specializing in information about NDR.

At the same time as this activity is occurring, community organizations, academics, and practitioners raise challenges to the advocates of state-sponsored NDR (Cain, 1984; Shonholtz, 1984; Auerbach, 1983; Abel, 1982a; Tomasic, 1982; Harrington, 1985, 1980; Santos, 1982; Kidder, 1981, 1980). They question, among other things, whether NDR is a threat to the protection and expansion of legal rights, whether it can achieve its stated claims, and the extent to which it represents a way of diverting attention from broader economic and social change. While some argue the irrelevance of NDR (Felstiner, 1974), or the imbalance of power between disputants (Auerbach, 1983), the deeper, more comprehensive criticisms emphasize its political character and ask questions about its contradictions, its relation to the state, and its meaning in the wider society (Baskin, 1984; Nader, 1984; Cain, 1984; Abel, 1982b; Spitzer, 1982; Santos, 1982).

But what would suggest that neighborhood dispute resolution (NDR) is anything other than it appears to be?[8] These dispute mechanisms are puzzling and contradictory. First, they involve a process that differs from the judicial system and yet they are bound up with the conventional system with respect to organizational ties, sources of referrals, and methods for handling similar problems. They are agencies of the state but without the trappings of the state and structurally independent. Second, the courts historically have been uninterested in and incapable of handling effectively minor neighborhood and family disputes (Sander, 1976; McGillis and Mullen, 1977). But the state now plans informal justice for this purpose—it formalizes informal justice. Third, population characteristics do not demonstrate a need for informal justice; there is no groundswell or demand for it from community residents (Merry, 1979; Harrington, 1980; Buckle and Buckle, 1982). Yet, ironically advocates espouse community values and Jeffersonian democratic rhetoric at a time and place when the community ideal as such is falsified by the reality of everyday life with its mobile populations and large urban centers (Auerbach, 1983; Merry, 1982b). Fourth, informalism appears to represent a con-

traction of state power, (e.g., the absence of formal rules, no authoritative officials, choice not to participate). But in other ways
its practices suggest an expansion of state power because of the
way it extends itself into areas of social life rarely touched by the
state (Abel, 1981; Santos, 1982). Fifth, these institutions seek to
make people aware of their conflicts as resolvable, and as problems requiring resolution at the same time as they desire to contain and suppress conflict. Sixth, informalism offers the possibility
for people to make new demands, based on conflicts within communities, while simultaneously remaining isolated from politics
because disputes are resolved individually and privately. Seventh,
some supporters of mediation speak of a need to create access to
justice—to meet unfulfilled demands for justice. Yet infomal dispute resolution is clearly not meant to dispense justice but only to
settle disputes (Abel, 1982b).

These contradictions raise questions. Why do informal mechanisms for dispute resolution reappear at this time with state support, given the historical possibility of other options (e.g., expansion of conventional courts to process more cases; creation of more
specialized courts; or expansion of other social service, political,
or private agencies to handle dispute settlement functions)? How
and why do interpersonal conflicts become a problem for state
intervention? Under what conditions? What definition of social
order does it offer?

Advocates for state-sponsored alternatives to courts and conventional legal processes share a number of assumptions about the
nature of disputes and social conflict, the role of the state, and the
definition of legal crisis (Goldberg et al., 1985; Ray and Clarke,
1985; NIDR, 1984; Folberg and Taylor, 1984; Alper and Nichols,
1981). These assumptions derive from a tradition which may be
referred to as liberal legal reformism that accepts the existing social order of power as a given and seeks limited, short-term solutions to practical problems. An overarching assumption is that a
rational response to social order is possible at each moment that
social problems are posed—that evolution and progress can resolve what, without an assumption of progress, may be a deeper
and less tractable problem for capitalist society.

Liberal legal reformism aspires to solve the problem of social
order through cooperation, administrative management of politi-

cal conflict, and impartial mediation between opposing classes. It views conflict as an evil to be avoided, absorbed, or resolved—all within the prevailing order. Only certain types of conflicts are acknowledged as legitimate in society (e.g., conflict between individuals, or interest groups, that does not challenge the fundamental right of capital to own and control the means of production). For example, a tenant may challenge an individual landlord's eviction or a rent increase. But the tenant cannot argue that the landlord (or landlords in general) cannot dispose of their property as they see fit. Tenants cannot base an argument on the needs of tenants or their perception that landlords do no work for their income. To the extent that class issues can be reduced to interpersonal ones, conflicts will be handled in some form. All other conflict must be managed by being translated into technical issues devoid of political content and isolated from more profound struggles or antagonisms that transcend the individual or limited group.

The major objective of conflict resolution, in this perspective, is not primarily justice but order-maintenance and problem solving. Formal legal procedures and authoritative judicial decision making obstruct the capacity to resolve a dispute; they merely impose a solution (Ford Foundation, 1978a; 1978b).

Crises with the judicial system are thus typically defined in managerial terms. Particular emphasis is placed on judicial overload and inefficiency, even though extensive research rejects the claims of "hyper lexis" (Galanter, 1983). Imperfections and inequalities in the social order are remedied by rules, due process, fairness, and social engineering techniques that ameliorate the consequences of conflict, guarantee equality of opportunity, and reduce the arbitrariness of law. Reformers, historically have been concerned with rooting out the arbitrary, corrupt character of the legal system by rules which ensure due process. But they have not sought justice, and seem to move toward informal alternatives to courts when the law "works" for disadvantaged social classes (Lazerson, 1982; Garth, 1982), when it is apparent that legitimacy may be undermined, or when the claims promoted challenge property relations and support new collective or individual rights (Reifner, 1982; Klare, 1982). Public officials, for example, seeking to increase the organizational efficiency of the judicial system, emphasize case overload, understaffing, delay, waste, and cumber-

some procedures (Ad Hoc Panel, 1984). They reject a more substantive conception of justice. At the same time, however, they
stress the threat to the legitimacy of the judicial system created by
unresponsive, costly, and ineffective courts.

Undoubtedly many citizens are dissatisfied with the quality of
justice (Currie, 1985). Few would dispute the value of flexibility,
informality, and responsiveness in dispute processing. Yet the instrumental and apolitical approach of the reforming liberal denies
the objective interests that generate social conflict by obscuring
those struggles that express class interests. Reformist analysis stresses
the benefits of mediation to individuals and measures the success
of these institutions according to the number of disputants who
reached agreements and were satisfied (Cook et al., 1980). This
interpersonal view of disputes ignores the ways in which individuals may benefit qua individuals but lose as members of a larger
social class whose interests cannot be fully satisfied through law
or private case-by-case resolution of personal grievances because
the issues involve questions of political power that extend beyond
legality. Reformist analysis thus prevents us from understanding
neighborhood dispute resolution forums as institutions of state social control by refusing to consider how conflict resolution may
relate to the underlying values, political structure, and the social
order of capitalist domination (Hay et al., 1975; Thompson, 1975;
Santos, 1982).

The liberal legal reformist perspective presents NDR as a solution to problems of managing the courts and expanding access to
the judicial system. It selects evidence for the success or failure of
these programs in a way that justifies its ideology, such as caseload, processing time, and disputant satisfaction (Alper and Nichols, 1981; Roehl and Cook, 1982; Merry, 1982a). Within this
framework no true evaluation of the programs can occur because
the evaluation excludes a social context that sets boundaries or
redefines the nature of the interaction between the parties in the
mediation process. The evaluation of such programs depends on
the interests that define the problems NDR addresses. If for example, NDR is evaluated according to the managerial conditions
which seemingly give rise to it (and the crisis produced by those
conditions, e.g., case overload), then evaluation becomes impossible. Either the variables measured are irrelevant except for the

managerial problem or the problem is of such generality that no particular instance or type of reform can be evaluated in terms of it (Merry, 1982a; Kidder, 1981).

Clearly much recent work on dispute resolution by anthropologists and legal sociologists is problematic precisely because the theoretical categories used to interpret conflict either lack reference to a cultural or political context external to the dispute process itself or overemphasize the individual and the dispute as the central units of analysis. Analysts have begun to provide alternative interpretations and question major assumptions about social conflict and judicial remedies (Kidder, 1981; Abel, 1982a; Santos, 1982; Harrington, 1982, 1985; Nader, 1984). Perhaps, most importantly, Maureen Cain and Kalman Kulcsar (1982) have challenged in some detail the "dispute processing paradigms" and their implications.

In capitalist societies disputes outside of marriage lack salience. Conflicts of interest which *are* salient are conflicts across class lines: between manufacturer, retailer, and consumer; between landlord organization . . . and tenant. . . . [to] insist that all these matters are disputes, and in some sense the same kind of thing as interpersonal quarrels, is analytically confusing if not dangerous.

[W]e simply plead for a conceptualization which starts from a theory of society, and which distinguishes between matters in theoretically relevant terms. . . . [I]nterclass conflicts are not most usefully conceived of as disputes . . . to do so obscures what may be special and important about the interpersonal events which possibly can be construed as disputes (1982: 388, 389).

How can we examine the contextual social process and relate it to neighborhood dispute resolution? How can we begin to create a more credible approach to judicial transformation characterized by the development of NDR?

What is needed is an analytical framework that can explain contemporary transformations in the regulation of social life from a nonmanagerial point of view—specifically, the management of social conflict by means of nonjudicial, informal administrative mechanisms. There are other perspectives which could be applied. Theories, influenced by the work of Durkheim, Weber, and Parsons, emphasizing the role of norms, values, and culture in the social control of economic resources represent one such possibility. Such approaches, although focused on the importance of the form of law and legal domination, tend to separate economic and political analysis and often fail to interpret the interests associated with a particular conception of social order (Unger, 1975). Social integration or cohesion represents a state of equilibrium (Parsons, 1949). The problem of disorder is related to modernity and the overrationalization of social life. An implicit critique of bureaucracy and advanced technology is apparent but does not adequately address issues of power nor systemic forces inherent in a corporate capitalist economy. No dialectic of resistance counters the universal tendencies within the bureaucratic form.

Another theoretical possibility can be derived from an analysis which stresses a decentralist, community-oriented, or even anarchist position, based on Jeffersonian or Rousseauian ideals, to explain trends toward informal, localized social processes (Schumacher, 1973; Morris and Hess, 1975; Lovins, 1977; Sale, 1980; Boyte, 1980).

In this perspective, scale is a central issue as well as an explanatory variable in understanding the restructuring of institutions toward smaller geographic or functional units. Decentralization is represented as an antidote to the overrationalization of society, social complexity, and the loss of control over daily life. It rarely connects its categories of thought to issues of power except in a general way and offers no particular distinctions between citizen-initiated and state-initiated attempts at decentralization of given institutions. Neither of these positions has been fully developed theoretically to provide a full-scale critique and derivation of informal dispute resolution that can be tied to class conflict or the material basis of production in a capitalist economy.

In his preface to *A Contribution to the Critique of Political Economy*, Marx states:

Neither legal relations nor political forms could be comprehended . . . by themselves or on the basis of a so-called general development of the human mind . . . on the contrary they originate in the material conditions of life. . . . In the social production of their existence, men invariably enter into definite relations, which are independent of their will, namely relations of production appropriate to a given stage in the development of their material forces of production ([1859] 1970b: 20).

A framework for interpreting the origin and significance of neighborhood dispute resolution that emerges out of a Marxist tradition can offer a more adequate explanation than that provided by liberal legal reformism or other functionalist perspectives. It relates judicial institutions to the foundation of political power in American capitalism—the organization of labor and capital. Transformations in the relations of production, work processes, ideologies, cultural life, the social environment, and institutions of crisis management, constitute basic components in such an analysis. In this perspective, class conflict is central. Whereas liberal legal reformism takes conflict between interest groups or even individuals as its basic analytical category, a perspective grounded in a Marxist framework identifies the struggle between antagonistic classes, specifically capital and labor, as a basic form of conflict—and one that cannot be resolved within capitalism. Such an analysis is not a crude materialism nor one which separates base from superstructure. On the contrary, material life and ideology are inextricably interrelated.

In short, this perspective presents the foundations for a critical analysis of NDR and the basis for a critique of liberal ideology and the programs themselves. It views the management of the labor process and social life in the community by capital and the state as two sides of the same problem and the resistance of labor to capitalist domination in general as a central theme. Such a presentation reformulates the politics of neighborhood dispute resolution as a mediated expression of class needs—capital constituted against labor. It demonstrates a connection between capital-labor relations (in the workplace and in urban communities) and neighborhood mediation forums. These forums are then understood as creating organizational relationships or forms which potentially defuse political grievances and legitimate the state to the public, disorganize community action, and manage social populations—at the same time as they offer a basis for an oppositional politics.

I will argue that the movement toward interpersonal, informal, decentralized mechanisms for dispute resolution organized through the judicial apparatus can only be understood fully when analyzed within a political and economic analysis of American capitalism, particularly the way in which its crises influence the form of the state. It can then be discussed as an ideological component of state power. More important, NDR can be identified not as an alternative or complement to courts but as an alternative to politics and community organizing.

There are three tasks in elaborating on this thesis. The first is to explain the derivation of NDR from class conflict, the social relations of production, and crises in the management of social life by the capitalist state. There is no way to demonstrate a direct connection between capitalist power, class struggle, and the details of NDR. Its meaning is therefore derived indirectly by examining the conditions under which it arises, its location within the state, and the ways in which its processes represent political domination. The second is to explain why NDR is a new form of the state and why it takes the particular form that it does. Third, is to demonstrate how it penetrates community social life and potentially contains political and social disorder in a manner determined by but disguised within its form as an apparatus of the state. At the same time we must show how it is bound to change and the contradictions that lead people to resist NDR.

My analysis proceeds as follows: the next five chapters outline central features of contemporary American capitalism, focusing on its contradictions, the antagonisms between capital and labor, the crises produced by these contradictions and struggles, and the role of the state. Attention is then directed to crises in the reproduction of the social order, the limitations of conventional forms of the state (including the judicial system), the nature of hegemony and hegemonic crises, and the ways in which restructuring in the state emerge from crisis and class conflict. My objective is to present a characterization of American capitalism within which NDR is embedded. It establishes the political, economic, and ideological context within advanced capitalism and situates NDR within the judicial apparatus of the capitalist state. By examining the changing nature of the state, and its developing forms, the shift toward NDR can be better understood.

The succeeding chapters (6 and 7) first explore who plans NDR and why and then consider how neighborhood dispute resolution forums engage people and manage their conflicts, and how hegemony operates in an institutional process to regulate social life. I explore both the rhetoric of NDR and its method. The analysis discusses the contradictions of NDR processes and why they are not solutions to problems of social order and class conflict.

In the course of the research, over a period of six years, I visited six mediation programs in Florida, California, New York, and Massachusetts; sat in on three mediation sessions; and interviewed project directors, mediators, and intake counselors in each. I also interviewed these same categories of mediation staff members by telephone in another eight programs. Their cooperation was in most cases contingent on anonymity, and therefore their names have not been listed in an appendix. Each quotation from staff members, with two exceptions, is from a different person. Some of the interviews were conducted for research purposes other than this book.

The mediation sessions which I attended were all of a similar nature in format. A mediator sat behind a desk in a barely furnished room with four or five chairs. The disputants would enter the room and sit a few feet apart facing the mediator or at the opposite ends of a table with the mediator in the center. The sessions typically lasted from one to two hours without a break. The mediators introduced themselves and offered very brief explanations of the process—the objectives, the mediator role, how they would proceed, and possible outcomes. Throughout the sessions, disputants violated the procedures numerous times, for example, speaking out of turn or seeking to prove they were right and therefore entitled to a "victory" rather than settlement. All of the mediation staffs I interviewed were friendly and cooperative. In general, they supported mediation and viewed it as a helpful alternative to courts for the disputants.

During mediation sessions, I examined the character of the interaction among all participants, the language or discourse, the presentations by mediators, as well as the mood and setting. Apart from interviews and attendance at these sessions, I also examined the rules of mediation by studying mediator training manuals or documents used to instruct mediators, project evaluations, program materials explaining mediation to the public, case studies, mediation transcripts; case histories; and congressional testimony. My objective in evaluating this material was to discover how mediation is expected to work, how planners and practitioners interpret mediation, and how people experience mediation as practiced.

This work provides a social theory for interpreting NDR by theorizing the conditions for its emergence and considering the relationship between changes in the structure of the state and the central features of mediation. The empirical material, however, is not to be interpreted as either case studies, anecdotes, or an attempt at ethnography. Rather, the program descriptions and evidentiary matter should be understood as providing a sense of how mediation works in a generic way. The material is thus suggestive and illustrative. Whichever program is considered, wherever one enters the analysis, and at whatever time, the same principles apply and indicate the fundamental nature of NDR. The central theme can only be demonstrated indirectly by exploring anamolies and contradictions, and by showing the relation between NDR's characteristics and the crises in the social order to which they partially respond.

NOTES

1. Richard Abel (1982a) indicates that legal institutions are informal "to the extent that they are nonbureaucratic in structure and relatively undifferentiated from the larger society, minimize the use of professionals, and eschew official law in favor of substantive and procedural norms that are vague, unwritten, commonsensical, flexible, *ad hoc*, and particularistic" (vol. 1, p. 2).

2. Mediation is a structured, informal process whereby a neutral third party (the mediator) assists the disputants to reach a voluntarily negotiated settlement of their conflict by developing options. Mediators encourage settlement, but have no power to render a decision.

3. The term neighborhood justice center technically refers to three experimental dispute resolution projects established by the Law Enforcement Assistance Administration in 1978. In this book I use the terms neighborhood dispute resolution, alternative dispute resolution, mediation, and informal dispute resolution interchangeably to refer to a broad range of nonjudicial, informal, state-funded or organized neighborhood dispute forums and processes, existing or potential, that seek to resolve interpersonal civil or criminal disputes. The term also refers to the types of dispute resolution, such as mediation or arbitration, that occur within these forums.

4. In 1920 the Jewish Conciliation Board was established in New York City (Fisher, 1975). Current interest in the concept can be traced to Fuller (1971), Danzig (1973), Fisher (1975), and Sander (1976), all of whom wrote widely read articles advocating alternatives to courts and proposing organizational models. Many of these models relied on approaches and techniques common to labor disputes.

5. Some of the more notable and well-researched dispute resolution forums include the Dispute Resolution Centers Program of the Unified Court System of the state of New York, the Neighborhood Justice Center of Atlanta, Inc., and the dispute settlement programs sponsored by the Office of the State Court Administrator in Florida. For a detailed list of programs and projects see Ray et al., 1986.

6. Funds were never appropriated because of the president's budget-cutting priorities for fiscal 1981. The act established a Dispute Resolution Resource Center within the Office for Improvement in the Administration of Justice in the Department of Justice. By surveying and evaluating experimental programs, the resource center, in its first year of activity, would have functioned as a clearinghouse for the exchange of information and provided technical assistance to those who wished to improve or create dispute resolution mechanisms. Its research would have been used to establish national priorities and guidelines. In each of its second through fifth years, the Resource Center had an authorization of ten million dollars, out of which it was to make grants to any nonprofit organization, business, bar association, or municipal agency for the purpose of improving or creating dispute resolution mechanisms.

7. See also Freedman, 1984. Interview with Lawrence Freedman, American Bar Association, August, 1986.

8. This book explores interpersonal neighborhood conflicts: those between friends, neighbors, family members, consumers and merchants, landlords and tenants. Most of these are handled within NDR centers or agencies connected with the courts. However, these conflicts represent only a small proportion of the types of conflicts handled by mediation-related services. Mediation is used for environmental, civil rights, educational, prison, medical, business, agency rule-making, and numerous other institutional and complex multiparty disputes.

PART I

CLASS STRUGGLE, CRISIS, AND THE CHANGING ROLE OF THE STATE

CHAPTER 1

Capitalism and Crisis

Neighborhood dispute resolution activities are institutions of crisis management and social control within the capitalist state. They cannot be explained in isolation from their connection to the state nor to the crises within the social order resulting from the social relations of capitalism. They create a mediating link between people and labor markets, labor processes, and consumption patterns within a given social environment. That link through the state represents a new form of the state in sustaining social order. It occurs at a moment of transformation in the productive relations of capitalism in managing social order. More than merely institutions of order maintenance, these activities and programs are political mechanisms that produce a system of meanings and practices connected to the management of a corporate capitalist economy, and are dependent on coordination and consensus. However, the ties of NDR to real community life, embedded in ideologies of self-management and local autonomy, semiautonomous from the formal state, create a potential for emancipatory practices that make their final effects undeterminable.

In order to demonstrate these propositions and their implications, neighborhood dispute resolution must be placed in a social context that includes not merely the immediate, local terrain in which it operates, but the class conflicts that shape its boundaries (Cain and Kulcsar, 1982). A theory of social order and disorder in American capitalism is required. Thus, before examining specific features of NDR, the contradictions and crises of capitalism are explored as a way to derive a general rationale for social regulation and examine the location of crisis. The role of the state is then considered since NDR is situated within the state. Here, I consider the forms of the state, the crises in its formal apparatuses, and the crises or impasses in its hegemonic ideologies. Finally, the emerging central characteristics of the state provide a prelude to understanding why NDR arises in its particular form at this historical juncture.

CAPITALISM AND CLASS STRUGGLE *(Mode of Production)*

A capitalist system is defined by the separation of the producers of value from the control of the means of production and capitalist control over the means of production. A central feature of American capitalism is the unending effort by the social class that owns and controls the apparatus of production to increase the rate of capital accumulation and to maintain control over the surplus produced by labor (Marx [1867] 1967). Sustaining capital expansion, extracting the surplus from labor, and realizing its value requires a variety of conditions—including a minimum of increased productivity, a flexible infrastructural environment, and the productivity of labor exceeding the amount necessary for its reproduction. These conditions are not automatically secured but depend on the outcome of an unresolvable class struggle between capital and labor.

Class antagonism in the capitalist mode of production, meaning the way in which the labor process is organized within a given set of social relations, emerges from the effort to expand the ratio of unpaid labor relative to paid labor. This is the meaning of exploitation. Expansion requires the exploitation of labor within a system of commodity production and exchange, subordinating their claims to organize and control production. At the same time, capital expansion also depends on the reproduction of labor. This class struggle, in which the capitalist class defends its control over the surplus produced by labor and labor resists—the most fundamental structural conflict in capitalist society—is a primary dynamic of social change. The social relations of production that arise from the economic and political struture of capitalism, based on these struggles, are formally expressed through the state (described in the following sections). The outcome of class struggles depends on historically specific conditions.

Capitalism is beset by a peculiar series of contradictions. These contradictions, resulting from incompatible imperatives within the system itself and class struggle, create crises that place absolute limits on capital expansion and the ability of capital to dominate labor. The resulting crises generate disruptions to the social order which influence the restructuring of capital, labor, and the institutions within the state that manage social conflict.

The most central contradiction of capitalist society is between the socialization of the forces of production, meaning their public, social character and consequences, and the private ownership and appropriation of surplus value (Marx [1867] 1967; Godelier, 1973). As capital expands, it expands the productive power of labor and concentrates and centralizes capital. Total private control is impossible because the surplus produced must be partially used for social investments such as housing, transportation, and health care. In order to deploy a labor force anywhere in society, productive activity must be integrated into all aspects of life to maintain the conditions of production and consumption. No mechanism exists to do this. This contradiction is expressed in the anarchic, unplanned, unregulated character of production which generates a further contradiction between production and consumption, creating a difficulty for capital to maintain its rate of profit. Capital is thus never able to provide a reliable, noncyclical economy to keep accumulation going without serious disruptions. For example, the disintegration within the steel industry creates instabilities in sectors that rely on steel. Large shifts in oil prices create havoc in whole geographic regions. When profits rise, however, capital often disinvests in the social infrastructure (e.g., housing), so that facilities needed for stable operations fail to get produced, also undermining capital expansion. As discussed later, this contradiction generates crises that hamper the circuits of capital. Thus, the possibilities of the productive forces are inhibited by the production relations because, in a capitalist society, the principal purpose of production is capital expansion rather than meeting needs or consumption (use values). The liberatory potential remains untapped. Moreover, capitalist development intensifies the interdependence of the productive forces and thereby creates difficulties in sustaining capital expansion on a broader scale, given the advancement in productive capacity. NDR bridges the gap at the surface between the disruptions arising out of these relations. It manages the expanding discord generated by dislocation and stress.

A second contradiction alluded to earlier concerns class struggle. Each class as a class has objective interests or imperatives. The survival of capitalism depends on reducing wage-labor to the status of a commodity, subject to market exchange relationships, and on reproducing labor as abstract labor, given that labor forms much of the basis for capitalist wealth. Capital cannot expand if labor interferes by having something to say about how labor is deployed. Yet capital cannot easily rely on an undifferentiated mass of labor power, since people form many attachments—to family, community, and craft, beyond loyalties to a company. To the extent that labor resists this reduction to commodity status, capital accumulation cannot occur in any regularized way. This is because the conditions for production are inherent in the relation that separates workers from the productive forces and exploits them—a relation that exists within and outside the productive system itself. Labor must therefore remain indifferent to this relation if it is not to undermine the system's basis.

Increase in relative surplus value means reducing necessary labor and relying on technological advancements, in contrast to expanding the working day. It is achieved by increasing worker productivity and reducing the cost of reproducing labor. Without an increase in productivity, capital expansion becomes impossible because labor is the primary basis of wealth. Predictability of the social order and uninterrupted production are essential. Capital must be able to organize the means of production without interference, invest freely in new means of production, create and dispose of property, and obtain access to raw materials. It must be able to move capital and labor quickly: to invest and disinvest at will.

Before stating labor's interest, it is important to explain what we mean, briefly, by the labor class as a class. That is, we must decide whether all wage-labor constitutes the labor class, industrial labor, or only productive labor. The definitions are fiercely debated (see Wright, 1978; Hunt, 1977). They are important because deciding how broadly labor is defined will determine how one interprets the scope of the crisis of social order capital must face—the organizational potential of the working class to disrupt capital accumulation, if not to relate to a class interest. I define the working class broadly to include all those categories of labor which sell their labor power for a wage, and do not own the means of production (Hunt, 1977). Class position is defined by the level of exploitation, not income or productivity. The implication of this definition is that, because labor refers to such a large category of workers beyond a traditional conception of the proletariat, social management becomes more difficult as capital expands.

At one level, labor, so far as its position in the productive process is to bear labor to a market—to sell labor power for a market-determined price—must maintain control over its own productive labor. It must control the surplus value it produces, the social conditions of its existence, both in the workplace and outside, while limiting its reduction to an instrument of production. The more control labor has, the less likely will it be exchanged for machinery or exploited. This represents its long-run class objectives, as a class diametrically opposed to capital. Labor, as abstract socialized labor in capitalist society, requires production for socialized collective consumption. This means production for need rather than market exchange and the expansion of the range of commodities and services available for such collective consumption—for example, health care, public mass transportation, social services, utilities, housing, education, and clean air and water. Increased wage rates, reduction in the cost of living, and an increase in the collective living space constitute its central interests. In the workplace, the same principle applies: individuals reduced to being adjuncts of machines and functioning under onerous conditions seek to control the work process in ways that they cannot always articulate. In the community, labor must have control over the essentials of daily life and access to basic social services. Labor, in resisting capital, also develops a unity, not a unity of spirit but of social consumption—surplus capital used not just for state benefits but for real control of private capital: what gets produced, where capital is invested, organizing the labor process. That is, undermining property is the final goal, not merely obtaining state benefits. For those who sell their labor power in a capitalist society, whatever their differences in historical experience or culture, all must handle the circumstances arising from the labor market power of capital that threatens them with unemployment, mechanization, and reduced living standards. Their common interests as participants in a capitalist labor process are thus to maintain control over the organization of labor. They all share such an interest in being emancipated from commodity status, whether they can verbalize it or not, independent of their immediate consciousness of this commonality. This interest exists to the extent labor must reproduce the conditions of life.

Labor must be understood as an autonomous force in itself and not simply subsumed under the logic of capital, although its existence within capitalism partially creates that autonomy. It possesses its own oppositional cultural logic (Aronowitz, 1981; 1985). Thus, labor has imperatives in bearing its labor power to the market that derive from its constitution as a class struggling with capital, and a productive force within capital. People have a subjective, cultural life within these processes. They express desires and engage in creative activities that clash with capitalist rationality, such as work discipline, conformity, and authority. For example, people may refuse incentives to work more and choose leisure (Aronowitz, 1985). This makes the outcome of class struggle unpredictable and contingent.

Labor resistance contains two essential elements: resistance to capital and self-development independent of capital. The reason labor can never be fully dominated by capital is that labor is not like other commodities: it cannot be separated from its owner. It does not exist to become a commodity and therefore has subjectivity, for example, to refuse to work. The greater the extent to which labor is reduced to a commodity the more labor resists. The greater the autonomy of labor, the more capital development is undermined. While people have always resisted domination (Thompson, 1966), nevertheless, resistance under capitalism takes a particular form (Burawoy, 1979; Edwards, 1979). It must be understood as the resistance of a socialized labor force in the interests of its own socialization, connected to use values, and vested in everyday life in the community. Labor is thus not to be understood as disparate individuals but as different communities which must have resources for cultural development. These common resistances generate community and they respond to the ordering of capital, not a generalized domination. Cultural resistances remain unpredictable because the cultural and political forms that arise in capitalist production and consumption processes are already constrained by those processes. Traditional forms of domination through the market, the political party, or the state become ill equipped to handle what appears irrational from the point of view of capital. NDR enters the social life of communities at a time when the unpredictability of social and cultural life expands with the increasing movements of capital in and out of communities.

A THEORY OF CRISIS

Crises occur in capitalism because its survival depends on contradictory imperatives (Habermas, 1975; Offe, 1984). The central crisis of capitalism is class struggle. Such struggle sets a barrier to expansion as the power and productivity of labor expand. James O'Connor argues that "crisis tendencies are not the result of systematic contradictions of capitalism, but originate in the emancipatory practice of human beings" (1981b: 324). They arise on the one hand, from working–class needs for subsistence and limits of the system's ability to produce surplus value. That is, labor resists efforts to be reduced to a commodity, struggling against the law of value, and subsumption under the law of exchange. But, on the other hand, crises emerge from the culture and social practices that define people outside the context of productive processes that cannot be subsumed under them (Aronowitz, 1981).

Even though some struggles can be understood within a logic of capital and its structures, the different crises between internal/external and systemic/social are all socially and politically created. The fundamental constraint on accumulation is resistance to exploitation in the different circuits of capital, based on the character of the specifically capitalist mode of production and the requirement to reproduce surplus value. This exploitation creates political practices which weaken existing institutional structures. The social crisis of capitalism must be understood in its totality. While crises begin with the arena of production, crises occur in all aspects of social life, in all circuits of capital, even though we distinguish them analytically. Thus they cannot be reduced to economic crises in "the last instance." And there is nothing inevitable about their outcome.

The class struggle as crisis is expressed as disruptions to order necessary to reproduce the conditions for accumulation. "Reproduction is the method by which the total social 'ensemble' including modes of circulation, distribution, and consumption is protected and repeated through time" (Dear, 1981: 482). Disruptions can be direct or indirect, long-term or short-term. Order in capitalism is a form of rationality that contradicts everyday life and working-class culture and values. Thus, disorder exists inherently in everyday life. Essentially, the crisis occurs in social reproduction—in the need to obtain coordination and consensus within a system based on anarchic production and within a form of rationality that negates the possibility of consensus in nonmarket terms.

In order to understand the idea of crisis more concretely, we need to consider how the anarchic character of capitalism creates a political contradiction and thereby a crisis: the drive to expand disintegrates communities, even though stable communities (the infrastructural environment) are a necessary condition of accumulation.

It is a problem related to social reproduction and uneven economic development. Local transactions, everyday social life and relations of reciprocity, the level at which NDR operates, come into contradiction with relations based on exchange and the general expansionary character of capitalist development (Lefebvre, 1976). Uneven development, such as wealth in one region and poverty and unemployment in another, occurs because expansion does not take place within the economy as a whole in any given historical period. When one sector expands others contract, limiting support for investment. Thus the logic of everyday personal life at the local level *and* the logic of an expanding, intrusive, interpenetrating capitalist development are incompatible.

The original, indigenous process of reproduction and of social cohesion becomes more and more undermined by the anarchy of commodity relationships and thus is itself increasingly characterized by crisis. At the same time, the capitalist form of productive development leads to . . . [the] destruction of the natural bases of production and reproduction in general (Hirsch, 1981: 596).

For example, the small business owner who wants stability and a guarantee that costs will be stable does not want a wildly fluctuating market. Another example is a tenant whose interest is stability of residence in conflict with a landlord whose expanding rate of profit is part of the logic of capital expansion—the landlord may want to tear down the building and replace it with another. "Capitalist development has therefore to negotiate a knife edge path between preserving the exchange values of past capital investments in the built environment and destroying the value of these investments in order to open up fresh room for accumulation" (Harvey, 1981: 113). To state capital's problem another way: how can stable reproductive formations and traditional settlement patterns be maintained which must be continually destabilized by capital expansion?

The expansion process is always expanding against something—which is stability and consolidation of primary relations or social connections among individuals and domestic community organization. Family life and community life are disrupted by labor mobility and the failure of communities to provide security. Capital must make people tolerate an expansion that is not in their interest as workers, human beings, or as residents of a neighborhood or settlement. The success or failure of their relations as such depends on the stabilization and integration of the local economy. This is also true for the community as a whole. And capital can only expand to the extent that it can draw labor power from the people who live in those communities. The capacity to perform labor is a problem of social reproduction. Labor power is useful only if it can be delivered to a market. And it can only be delivered to a market and exploited if the bearers of labor power have a stable, noncapitalist existence—that is, a stable community, a settlement-oriented existence.

But labor cannot be stabilized if capital expansion proceeds competitively as it does. Where capital creates corporate centers and capital intensive development occurs, it reduces industrial jobs and displaces blue-collar workers, thereby disrupting community life. Sometimes capital must disorganize social life and disinvest in communities because accumulation partly depends on the capacity to move capital and labor quickly. Capital is not committed to the well-being of communities or individuals. Plant closings and capital shifts testify to this, as well as activities by banks such as redlining and refusal to invest in a community. Equally important, in a political sense, austerity may be a goal to weaken the work force and destabilize its organizational power. The need for predictability and order for capital can therefore also mean planned disorder for people and communities. But there are limits. This is a contradiction: the need to expand and thereby vitiate communities and to maintain communities at the same time.

Let us now consider the way in which class struggle at the level of the labor class creates a crisis of order that requires social regulation. The process of reproduction—to perpetuate the working class and its class position, and to disorganize it politically—is not inevitable or automatic. As I make clear in the discussion of the state, it requires apparatuses which monitor everyday life and contain disruption. Social control is inherent in class struggle itself, though not necessarily consciously imposed because expansion and the extraction of surplus value is based on exploitation (Braverman, 1974; Hirsch, 1978). However, it is not only because labor is a factor of production but because labor is forced to sell itself to capital that the use of labor requires that it submit to capital. Thus the order that arises in capitalist society as a result of class struggle is not random, natural, inevitable, or an outcome of a logical need for order. Rather, a particular kind of order emerges, partially geared to the mode of production, partly distinct from it. How is capitalist order distinct from order required in any social formation?

David Gartman (1978), David Gordon (1976), and Richard Edwards (1979) all distinguish between the necessity for *some* type of order, authority, and coordination in any system of production and the control mechanisms under capitalism. Each recognizes that the worker-capitalist relation is not the automatic result of market forces or the natural attribute of human beings. Because labor seeks to limit the extent of its exploitation by capital, capital must use what Gartman calls "surplus control" to compel labor to work under conditions that it would not ordinarily accept if it were organizing the work process. "Surplus control, in contrast with basic control, increases the rate of surplus value solely because it represses the resistance of an exploited class" (Gartman, 1978: 103).

Gordon's distinction between quantitative and qualitative efficiency in a capitalist economy helps to elaborate the notion of surplus and basic control. Quantitative efficiency means that producers in any social system seek to generate the greatest output for the least input (the object of Gartman's "basic control"). But qualitative efficiency (the goal of Gartman's "surplus control") refers to a productive process "that best reproduces the class relations of a mode of production . . . maximizes the ability of the ruling class to reproduce its domination . . . and minimizes producers' resistance to such domination" (Gordon, 1976: 22).

Edwards also examines the issue from the perspective of labor resistance but reminds us that labor is not a commodity like other commodities. Capital purchases *labor power*—the capacity to perform labor. But capital must find special mechanisms to extract *labor*. "Control is rendered problematic because, unlike other commodities . . . labor power is always embodied in people, who have their own interests and needs and who retain their power to resist" (Edwards, 1979: 12). Hence, the mechanisms of social control are transformed as labor resists and as capitalists attempt to overcome impediments to capital expansion and extract the surplus. Yet control is made difficult by the changing terrain of class struggle, as the mode of production develops historically.

Social control is itself contradictory and dialectical. This contradiction stems from capital's dual obligation: to sustain property relations—the system of exchange, the free flow of goods and services—while maintaining the circulation and well-being of the labor force. The regulation of any one of these realms involves the other. Capital must maintain the work force outside the workplace and also individuate or fragment the work force so that it can sell its labor power as free, unattached labor. Thus, for every instance of control there is an instance of socialization and therefore resistance to control, even if not an organized resistance. That is, control brings people together and provides the experience of social life that constitutes a possible basis for progressive social movements in a way that challenges control but also removes the connection between individual conflicts and public issues. For example, E. P. Thompson (1966) demonstrates how the strict supervision, rigorous discipline, and doctrinaire normative structure of eighteenth-century methodism seemingly

appears as a politically regressive, or "stabilizing influence" . . . [However], methodism was indirectly responsible for a growth in the self-confidence and capacity for organization of working people. [According to Southey] "methodism has familiarized the lower classes to the work of combining in associations, making rules for their own governance." Throughout the early history of methodism we can see a shaping democratic spirit (42).

Why must this contradiction persist? To the extent that social control is capitalist control, labor must be dominated but also protected in order to extract labor from workers. Production requires coordination and cooperation among workers, at the same time as capitalists seek control over production. Although capitalists possess a great capacity for exercising control, the long-term outcomes of those controls cannot be prejudged. Moreover, the particular systems of control that emerge are based on struggles between capital and labor, however indirect. They cannot be understood as either rationalizations that correspond to an abstracted need for efficiency or the capability to discipline inherent in modern technologies. The analysis of state social control, then, is not a critique of social control per se, but an interpretation of class power that generates its particular content and forms (Fine, 1979a).

The social crises in advanced capitalism are crises that concern control of unanticipated consequences of the socialization of labor and the resistances that labor offers. NDR is an institution of the state within that struggle. Because of its structural design features (emanating from hierarchical institutions within the state) and its process (a type of rationality alien to the community), its relations of authority cannot be understood as indigenous to the community. Rather, its processes of decision making impose a level of formal rationality on interpersonal relations that cannot be associated with any social movements not identifiably connected to the state, even though it appears as an autonomous organizational innovation. Later I will explore NDR as a state institution of social crisis management that deals with those volatile, disruptive elements in society that cannot be contained by traditional political arrangements or ideological appeals. But before exploring the role of the capitalist state and the nature of crisis at that level, we need to consider contemporary crises in accumulation and the social order, apart from the state, that exacerbate the general crisis that arises from the contradictions of capitalism.

CONTEMPORARY CRISES: LABOR

The inherent crisis tendencies within capitalist society are heightened at certain historical junctures in capitalist development. They exist prior to their manifestation in the state. For example, there are crises resulting from the restructuring of capital, from labor struggles, from nonlabor social movements and resistances, and from changes and disruptions in urban environments where new forms of the state such as NDR develop.

Capital expansion depends on endless and increasingly rapid restructurings and uneven development. The increasing centralization and concentration of capital, for example, a basic form of restructuring, means that crisis in one sector of the economy affects the entire economy—witness the result of plant shutdowns by large corporations, small changes in the interest rate, and production stoppages in major industries. Moreover, the interdependence of the global economy and the inability of the United States politically to dominate other capitalist and developing nations diminish the access of capitalists to cheap labor, raw materials, and new markets. Investments are riskier, and other capitalist nations such as Japan invade U.S. markets. Competition leads to expansion of technologies which expand again the amount of investment and the level of risk. Corporate debt, third world debt, and rising interest costs have periodically limited expansion and threatened the health of the financial system. Some corporations, for example, cannot generate enough capital for investment without excessive borrowing, and the economy cannot easily absorb the expanded credit.

These restructurings and the impediments to expansion they generate lead to more direct exploitation of labor. The increase in exploitation means increased resistance by labor. The management of social life, always in flux, becomes more encompassing and more difficult with each restructuring.

24 Changes in the composition of the work force, labor markets, and the social organization of the work process present monopoly sector capital with obstacles, especially in the extraction of surplus value. The work force is less homogeneous than in earlier historical periods. Workers possess more diverse skills than previously. The interdependent character of production and the increased size of the wage and salaried labor class reduce the ability of capital to

manage the labor force effectively. Different segments of the labor force require different forms of control, creating a problem in co-ordination. The expanded labor force produces more individuals with common economic interests and thus a greater potential to oppose capital, even though it is less physically concentrated geo-graphically.

Moreover, an increasing proportion of the labor force is em-ployed in the service sector and by the state (Fox et al., 1981). Many of these workers are either nonproductive or only produce surplus value indirectly. They include workers involved in admin-istration, finance, sales, maintenance, and inspection. Their pro-ductivity cannot be evaluated by the same means as that of work-ers who are directly involved in production. State workers are organizing more rapidly than those in other sectors, and their unions tend to be especially militant (Johnston, 1981). They have not es-tablished fixed bargaining patterns, and the demand for their labor is more a function of political considerations than of market con-ditions.

Struggles with labor, competition among capitalists, advances in technology, and the drive to expand production require con-stant innovations in the organization of work (Hirschhorn, 1978). But because of the sophisticated technological base and large scale of the more centralized industries, the retooling required by tech-nological innovation cannot be accomplished quickly. For exam-ple, enterprises cannot switch easily between labor-intensive and capital-intensive production. Job training takes longer. "The qual-ity of labor power must necessarily be raised in all capitalist econ-omies to match the increased sophistication of production and its attendant social processes" (Gough, 1972: 53).

The continuous transformation of labor creates instabilities in managing the labor force as a whole. The integrated, interdepen-dent character of the labor process requires workers in some in-dustries to understand more about the entire process in order to perform their jobs, thus reducing their dependence on the capital-ist to control production. The more knowledge workers have, the more capable they become to make decisions about the organiza-tion of work, particularly its pace and content. This generates a contradiction. Capitalists must maintain control of production and desire to deskill workers in order to manage them more effectively. But capital expansion depends on innovation which in turn depends on increasing the skills of workers.

There are also numerous challenges to capitalist domination of labor in the labor process. First, workers resist controls over the pace of production, work rules, job classifications, and layoffs; they seek open corporate ledgers; they assert their rights on the shop floor and challenge management's investment decisions and prerogative to introduce new technology (Noble, 1978; Shaiken, 1979). They also demand greater job security and protective benefits as the economy becomes more unstable and inflation and unemployment rise simultaneously. Recently, workers have begun to consider ways of controlling the investment of their pension funds and of taking over plants that capital wishes to shut down (Carnoy and Shearer, 1980; Zwerdling, 1980). Second, workers demand better health and safety conditions, especially as the source of disease is traced to the workplace. Third, labor actively resists capitalist control through strikes, slowdowns, and sabotage. Absenteeism, turnover, and working to rule may also be considered forms of resistance. All of these resistances apply to white-collar as well as to manual labor (Johnston, 1981; Cummings and Greenbaum, 1978).

Finally, in the evolving world political economy, labor recognizes the need to become more involved in decisions affecting the nation as a whole—decisions that concern not only wages and benefits but also issues far more fundamental to the capitalist class than wages and benefits, such as the distribution of national income and the allocation of capital (Hymer, 1978). Thus, labor organizes collectively around issues such as foreign trade, tax reform, full employment, and energy policy, thereby expanding the scope of debate and escalating the scale of conflict. André Gorz best expresses the general problem of advancing the knowledge or capacities of the working class to expand capital while seeking to minimize the power of labor.

The necessity of developing human capabilities imposed by modern processes of production is in contradiction with the political necessity of ensuring that this kind of development of human capabilities does not bring in its wake any augmentation of the independence of the individual, provoking him to challenge the present division of social labor and the distribution of power (1972: 479).

Contemporary challenges to the distribution of power demonstrate the increasing artificiality in thinking about public and private power, or even work and community, as separate realms. The social environment in which NDR is physically situated, and where all types of conflicts occur, influences relations at work and in the environment. People seek to secure their well-being both in and outside the workplace. And there are direct connections between the work wage and the social wage. The conditions within a given industry and the existence of jobs within a community are deeply affected by state policy. More important, disruptions to capital accumulation occur at a prepolitical level (e.g., health conditions, crime), as well as in the political realm, because capital penetrates all social spaces. Capitalist domination reaches those spaces as well. This prepolitical realm, however, cannot be regulated by market values.

CONTEMPORARY CRISES: URBAN ENVIRONMENTS

Most neighborhood dispute resolution centers, particularly those funded or sponsored by the state, are established in urban environments. They handle cases which arise from the stresses of urban life (Felstiner and Williams, 1978). Despite some production shifts to suburban and rural areas, urban environments still remain central production sites, markets, investment sites, and administrative control centers for capital (Gregory and Urry, 1985; Badcock, 1984; Harvey, 1981; Gordon, 1977; Mollenkopf, 1977). These urban centers—and their labor power, roads, schools, services, and communications—must be organized so as to create the preconditions for production, exchange, and investment. The city is essential to capitalist reproduction. As physical space, the city must be considered part of the means of production. But under almost any conditions, capital finds difficulty in regulating noncommodity production: the infrastructural environment in urban areas.

Since the 1960s the role of the urban environment as a "support center" for capital has changed dramatically. Although production in the monopoly sector has in many locales moved out of the central city to areas where taxes are lower, land is cheaper, and workers are less organized, smaller, competitive industries are left behind that lack the resources to move and depend on the local client population for revenue. The sporadic labor needs of the latter lead to an increase in the numbers of unemployed, underemployed, and poorly paid (O'Connor, 1984; Hill, 1976; Gordon, 1977).

Urban decay, congestion, and unemployment threaten overall capital accumulation. Growing, volatile, surplus populations produce social unrest and create the potential for collective action that disrupts production and challenges capitalist control (Brady, 1981). These populations have always posed a political threat, but the recent economic dislocations and the tensions produced change the magnitude and nature of that threat as surplus populations become larger and more permanent. The main threat to order does not come particularly from the tenured labor force and civil service, although, to be sure, they play a role—especially as they are highly mobile and not community oriented. Rather it comes from those groups who move in and out of the regular work force.

A problem of order arises not only because of a legal crisis but because of the characteristics and conditions of a peculiar kind of wage labor. As part of a reserve army of labor, they represent a volatile group, in part because they are less attached to community institutions. Perhaps equally important are the nonemployed—students, mental patients, and others under long-term care, such as prisoners and those who permanently drop out of the labor market. The population of this group is expanding rapidly as funds for social services decline. They will be forced back into a competitive labor market and the reserve army (Ehrenreich, 1981). Crises in social order occur partly because the subject matter, the details of everyday life connected to the expansion of capital and the extraction of the surplus also expand.

Interpersonal conflicts can sometimes be understood as disruptions—they disrupt the reproduction of labor power. Although these conflicts are not caused by capitalism per se many of them cause problems relative to an economic definition of labor. Since individuals are sources or bearers of labor power, interpersonal conflicts can potentially impair it, interfere with the reproduction of the labor force, maintaining it as a labor market, and pose difficulties for capitalist control. Why? Labor power is no longer to be understood as a collection of individuals within a workplace but as a total social infrastructure, reflecting an elaborated net-

work of capitalist production. The expansion of capital and technology recomposes the labor class as a society of production, not
individuals. Individuals are a member of a social infrastructure—
not just a labor market or some other economic entity. The availability of labor depends on the infrastructure: skills, technology,
and the social life of producers. Conflict is a disruption because it
impairs the reliability of infrastructural processes rather than disrupting the energy of labor. City life and the infrastructure make
labor possible, in contrast to its previous historical production in
the home or school. This infrastructure, being almost everywhere, becomes more important, more fragile, and vulnerable to
disruption, including localized conflicts. For example, landlord-
tenant disputes could potentially lead to challenges about the overall quality of housing or the ability of capital to invest in any
geographic area. From the perspective of reproducing labor, which
requires mobility and the regularity of movement in and out of
the labor force, landlord-tenant problems, such as evictions, could
create a volatile population not readily available or able to deal
with changes in the employment structure.

Such conflicts, which are the subject matter of NDR, reflect the
tensions of life as lived in capitalist society. For example, a conflict
between two neighbors in an apartment building about too much
noise made by one may really reflect the poor quality of housing
and the density of living conditions more generally. On the other
hand, certain interpersonal conflicts also respond to specific dislocations and scarcities as conditions of community life under capitalism. The need for a highly mobile labor force makes family life
problematic. Mobility produces shifts in individuals' lives which
destabilize social relations and put pressure on family and municipal budgets. This dislocation creates competition: the capital accumulation process finds its expression in property relations—over
housing, commodities, and so forth—that generate conflicts over
local budgets, civil rights, land use, and other local policies. These
conflicts could potentially lead to collective action for social change
or social disorganization that can destabilize the infrastructural
system within which production, exchange, and consumption occur.

Seemingly minor disruptions in the community (like those in

the workplace) may interfere with capital expansion, the extraction of surplus value, and the realization of capital.

As profits under capitalism have come to depend less on price competition and costs of production and more on maintaining monopolistic control over markets and elevating levels of demand, the cultivation of consumer habits, the creation of "consumption communities," and the shaping of consciousness itself have become the *sine qua non* of capitalist growth (Spitzer, 1979b: 199).

Mental and physical illness, family fights, alcoholism, drug addiction, neighborhood conflicts, and other "social problems" of urban society cannot be ignored by capitalists precisely because the social environment where disruption occurs has itself become a form of capital as new modes of production emerge (Hirschhorn, 1978). These problems can result in absenteeism and tension at work, thereby reducing productivity. The quality of so-called human capital declines. They also require increased social expenditures which can diminish the surplus available for capital.

Class struggle in the community takes two principal forms. First, in place of individuals merely seeking to consume more goods and services, we find collectivities demanding improvements in the environment, the quality of housing, or mass transportation. Second, community groups seek to expand control over a wide variety of subjects—energy, schools, city planning, community services, bank policies, land use, food distribution, urban renewal, and plant closings—thereby breaking down the artificial distinction between workplace and community. The worker and the citizen are the same person (Katznelson, 1981). These challenges clarify the opposition between the interests of capital and labor and can heighten worker consciousness of collective needs.

The neighborhood, consumer, welfare rights, women's, and environmental movements that arose in the 1970s generate new confrontations with capital, contributing to a "class-defined polarization" that parallels labor organizing and "seeks to form broader alliances of the powerless across lines of division like income and racial differences" (Boyte, 1979: 10). These forms of opposition by the working class and surplus populations are a partial response to the decay of the urban infrastructure contained in "threats to living standards, urban services . . . housing and other essentials of daily life" (Boyte, 1979: 10). They result from the unrelenting pursuit of economic growth that leads to intensification of land use for commercial purposes, highrises, and urban renewal, thereby disorganizing neighborhoods. Perhaps most important is that many responses were not merely reactive or focused on claims against the state but involved attempts to produce services in those areas where capital was failing—health care, food, and energy—thus drawing into question the inevitability of the capitalist mode of production (Boyte, 1979; Morris, 1982).

Many of these efforts failed. But they established a basis for community organizing and offered alternative models for both production *and* distribution (Morris and Hess, 1975). Many community organizations "have started to address themselves to the relationship between urban neighborhood deterioration and the flow of capital between urban centers and regions" (Drier, 1979: 12). As Ira Katznelson has noted, "School, welfare, police, and housing issues were treated together, as aspects of a total condition. As a result, authorities had to manage conflict that was much more intense and less susceptible to piecemeal solutions . . . "(1981: 121). Citizens reacted with hostility to public authority, particularly as local government acted with corporate capital to create unrestricted growth embodied in urban renewal and projects such as Westway in New York, convention centers, and other activities leading to massive displacement. Opposition was directed not just at the state but at capital directly—landlords, banks, and polluting businesses.

Organized protests involve the use of hearings, referenda, administrative review, and lawsuits and express the collective needs of communities at many bureaucratic levels. The fragmentation of local government sometimes restricts the capacity of capital to dominate the city because capital cannot identify a single decision maker from which it can extract the policies it needs at a macrolevel. The neighborhood dispute resolution center is a response to disorganize community challenges by demobilizing and absorbing demands at the individual level. If people take their claims to NDR, an unaccountable institution which treats conflicts on a case-by-case basis as private, interpersonal disputes, then building social movements could prove more difficult, especially as public claims decline and citizens rely on NDR rather than on their own community groups. Moreover, if people do not protest their problems in some public forum, then organized social change (through building consumer or tenant law, as well as in other ways that draw attention to the system-wide character of the issues) becomes more difficult.

CHAPTER 2

The Role of the Capitalist State

The role of the capitalist state is important to understanding NDR because the state represents a primary arena through which the conflicts between capital and labor and other nonclass forces are mediated and displayed. It is the central mechanism for sustaining the social relations of production when markets fail and when hegemonic controls in civil society weaken.

Modifications of state apparatuses such as informal justice occur as a result of the state's control over judicial institutions. Neighborhood dispute resolution centers are organizationally situated within the judicial system and represent an innovation. They are part of the state apparatus and absorb activities of other formal state apparatuses, such as the judiciary and the police, as well as perform new functions of social control. At an organizational level, NDR is an *agency* of the capitalist state. But the NDR center is more than an apparatus of the state. It is constituted by a system of practices and relations that extend into civil society. It represents an administrative form of the state and, at the same time, a new form of the state: a relatively new guise or appearance as nonstate.

In asserting that NDR is a new form of the state, we first need to consider what the state is and what it does. The state is a regulative form of public power, determined by class struggle, that derives its existence from the historical development of the capitalist mode of production and the social formation of capitalism. It is an institution of crisis management and an expression of class relations that mediates class contradictions. The state's overall objective is to secure the reproduction of capital in its long-term political imperatives. This means creating conditions necessary for capital accumulation as a whole. Thus the central feature of the state is its class character, even though it appears as neutral. However, because the state arises out of class struggle it cannot be fully dominated by capital's general interests. Its legitimacy is always indeterminate. But there is no automatic translation of capitalist power into state power. The state does not function for capital and must be understood as relatively autonomous from the circuits of capital, while simultaneously inherent in capitalist social relations. The social formation of capitalism transcends economic relations. But this relative autonomy creates as many problems as it solves for the state in securing the conditions for social reproduction.

The state, moreover, is not a separate institution distinct from society, but operates as part of the overall social formation of capital itself. Its boundaries remain fluid and difficult to discern. State structures are fragmented and contingent on historical conditions, and are connected to a particular mode of production. The state is therefore a set of processes and social relations that emerge from and are determined by class struggle within capitalist relations of production—rather than from any preconceived logic of capital (Offe, 1984; Poulantzas, 1968; Gramsci, 1971). As a form of class power, the state structures or mediates class relations. This power at any given moment is determined by the balance of class forces. There is no a priori unity of the state. Its elements must be politically created (Gramsci, 1971). In Nicos Poulantzas's terms, the state is itself an arena of class struggle between capital, labor and other social movements. The form that the state takes as an ensemble of institutions of representation and intervention is crucial for sustaining its capacity, at any given instance, to act on behalf of capital. That form is also determined by class struggle in general and, specifically, the way in which labor must be developed and extracted at any given moment within a mode of production.

NDR represents a change in the form of the state, based on identifiable crises. The general form of the state is its formal separation from the economic sphere—the circuits of capital. It remains outside the market and the law of value, an essential condition for reproducing the social relations of capital. Within this relation, its specific form is never fixed.

We can identify at least three basic functions or activities of the state, all of which overlap. First, the state creates the general conditions for capital accumulation. This includes providing infrastructural support, generating the material conditions for production and consumption, regulating exchange, and creating demand. The second is legitimation and social cohesion or social integration. This includes the maintenance and reproduction of the wage-labor force through schools, welfare, and other social investments, and ideological controls which fragment collective political action and absorb discontent. The third is hegemony, which includes the active creation of order and consensus necessary to sustain capitalist power and stability. All capitalist social relations are involved in the regulation of class conflict. Our concern is with the latter two.

The necessity of the state derives from the division of labor and the interdependencies produced by capitalist development. Such development destroys traditional forms of social life. The necessity for the state occurs too because the relations of capital require guidance and organized political regulation. There must be institutions which mediate capitalist power and the direct management of the social order, and also translate or process the interests of each class into structural forms that can execute them. Private capitals cannot do this. The market system cannot by itself socialize the work force, or sustain the conditions for accumulation, or reproduce class relations, given the disorganizing effects of capital accumulation on the population. Wage labor must be secured and protected simultaneously. An institutionalized steering mechanism guided by political rules must be created to connect production and exchange. In Jurgen Habermas's terms (1975), the system requirements of accumulation are in conflict with the values of the culture. To transform people into wage-labor is a necessary activity that only the state can perform, given that workers do not automatically submit to the imperatives of capitalist social relations. In sum, the conditions necessary for survival of capitalist social relations are incompatible with the logic of value or commodification. The state assumes these noncommodified activities by socializing the relations of production.

CONTRADICTION AND CRISIS IN THE FORMAL STATE

The capitalist state is a thoroughly contradictory institution. Its central contradiction occurs between its private objectives and its public appearances. If state measures are to appear as legitimate, the state must appear as neutral, universal, and autonomous.

Thus, the central crisis of the state occurs because it must violate its own premises, boundaries, legitimacy requirements, and rules in order to fulfill its role for capital, that is, to operate as a class state (Offe, 1984; Hirsch, 1978). The state cannot readily maintain its autonomy from the private sphere (Wolfe, 1977) because the state uses noncommodified systems to protect the commodity form (market relations and the law of value). Doing so interferes with capital's unrelenting efforts to reduce social life to the law of value, and to incorporate more aspects of social life under the commodity form as it expands. To the extent that the state encroaches on the private sector, the surplus available for capital is reduced, endangering its legitimation. State policies can thus restrict capital accumulation while trying to protect it. To the extent that administrative state power becomes dominant over exchange relations, a variety of social disorders and political challenges to capital are triggered. Accumulation becomes repoliticized.

In Claus Offe's terms, the question is whether "the political-administrative problem can politically regulate the economic system without politicizing its substance and thus negating its identity as a capitalist economic system based on private production and appropriation" (1984: 52). This happens as political intervention generates an idea of needs and use values that challenge the market system. Yet without such intervention, the market may collapse because it cannot meet the conditions for its survival.

One of the constraints imposed on governance in capitalist society concerns the capacity to maintain social order. To the extent that state action in the economy, for example, is compatible with the needs of capital as a class interest, it undermines the conditions for capital accumulation as a whole because it destroys the material conditions for production. And by acting for capital as a whole, it raises challenges from particular fractions of capital and subordinate classes (Miliband, 1973). Consensus can never be achieved because for capital to dominate as a class requires internal representation among numerous fractions, such as finance, industry, and real estate. At the same time, all subordinate social classes beyond these fractions would have to develop loyalty to capital's leadership. Thus, capital must continually suspend its own foundations to move forward (Jessop, 1983; Hirsch, 1978, 1981). Seeking to reproduce the working class, it sometimes strengthens it. And overexploitation can destroy labor's productive and consumptive capacity, as well as control over labor.

There has been a shift in the power, authority, and activities of traditional state institutions that mediate class conflict, preventing its emergence or escalation and otherwise channeling and absorbing discontent. They have become obsolete and ineffective for *capital*. These institutions, such as police, courts, prisons, schools, and mental institutions, some of which are still oppressive and powerful, may not adequately reproduce a politically docile, adaptable, finely honed, productive labor force for a variety of reasons. They represent blunt instruments which exclude, immobilize, ostracize, and otherwise repress people but do not always prepare, manage, or direct them in relation to the specific conditions demanded by labor markets and production processes.

Increasingly, formal state apparatuses have also had to accept more tasks as private institutions such as church and family have become inadequate to handle private and public disorder. Family fights, for example, prime subject matter for NDR, disrupt the worker qua worker and the community peace. Until the emergence of the monopoly phase of capitalist development, the dominant forms of control were notably impersonal, technological, and oriented toward objectifying social relations (Spitzer, 1979b). Such objectification created problems of legitimation because control presented itself as an alien force, separate from the community. For example, the rule of law can be particularly unresponsive, and state action that relies on it undermines state legitimacy (Unger, 1975). Although we find in the state many initiatives that move away from the rule of law toward generalized conflict resolution procedures, such as police crisis intervention units, there are tensions in these activities. Regulating community life is an important aspect of the police function, for example, handling disorderly conduct, vagrants, public drunkenness, and family fights (Spitzer, 1981; Cohen, 1985). But although police handle these activities and other moments of conflict, they cannot resolve, regulate, or prevent them or, in other ways, manage the social environment in accordance with the requirements for order in a capitalist society. The capacity of the police to respond to disruption with precise and intensive regulation is limited by legal procedure, police organization, and police distaste for order maintenance functions. The police are but one example of limits in a formal state apparatus that arise due to a shift in the nature of order and disorder in the social environment. The acceptable boundaries of discourse and behavior change, as do the capacities of the state to contain protest, absorb discontent, and incorporate marginal populations. Each modification creates new antagonisms. As a result, many of these institutions remain insufficient for handling disruption and conflict that either cannot always be defined as deviant behavior or treated with a solution tailored to the precise character of local conditions during periods of rapid change. Moreover, they remain unresponsive to the differences among numerous segments of marginal social populations.

A problem with most forms of direct or conventional state control is that people often resist, not only because it is imposed but because it is not theirs. As these traditional institutions penetrate more deeply into social life with additional proactive strategies and practices (e.g., police family crisis intervention units), the resistance becomes stronger. These institutions of control—state and nonstate—cannot meet the conditions for rationality, such as organizing the production process and its infrastructure, and for legitimation. They cannot handle disruptions exacerbated by new forms of competition, the politicization of issues, the restructuring of labor markets, and other forms of dislocation.

The formal state apparatuses represent only a minimal aspect of the state. For the state exists throughout the culture, embedded in social practices, activities, symbols, and ideologies. If we understand the state as a system of social relations that create order and maintain the rule of capital, we can begin to explore the way in which order is created in everyday life, absent the visible presence of a state apparatus. For a social class, such as capitalists, to dominate, it must exercise intellectual and moral leadership, whereby institutions and ideas establish power beyond purely organizational means or according to immediate economic interests. The limits of the formal state lead to modifications and transformations that have produced NDR.

CHAPTER 3

Hegemony, Social Reproduction, and the Role of the State

The contradictions of capitalism make it unstable as a social system. Formal state institutions, direct force, and direct appeals for regime support are never enough to justify power (Neumann, 1957). Other forms of political control are required. NDR emerges out of the particular struggles of a capitalist social order in constant change. The central argument is that NDR represents a relatively new aspect of the state related to a shift in the structure of the formal state and the limits of ideology.

A description of how domination operates or fails in an institution such as NDR requires a more general understanding of social reproduction. While I have explained the underlying object or content of reproduction, namely capital accumulation, and how capital requires a particular kind of social order to reproduce itself, reproduction itself needs to be explored.

In order to survive, capitalist rule must be secured and obscured without direct force and without the appearance of promoting direct class interests or indeed, any exercise of power. Apart from producing the conditions for expansion per se, it must also reproduce the social relations of production. This process, never guaranteed, is always in flux, as capitalism is always undergoing historical development. Moreover, people struggle to gain control over their lives; they resist exploitation and engage in oppositional behavior. Thus we need a way to examine the ideological nature of the state. For it is only by examining the social basis of state power and the way it promotes a view of reality that it becomes

possible to understand how the social relations of capitalism are
reproduced and change.

THE NATURE OF HEGEMONY

Antonio Gramsci's concept of hegemony (1971) is a useful start-
ing point for exploring the general nature of political control exercised by a social class and its representatives. For Gramsci, hegemony is a class relation that refers to the way in which order is
achieved and maintained within the entire range of social and political institutions in a society—not merely the economic mode of
production. It is a means for organizing consent in contrast to
direct use of force or bureaucratic domination. In Gramscian terms,
hegemony is contrasted with "rule," direct political or social force,
control, or indoctrination. It is a form of political and moral leadership or ideological domination. Raymond Williams explains how
hegemony involves

a saturation of the whole process of living . . . the whole substance of
lived identities and relationships. . . . It is a whole body of practices and
expectations over the whole of living: our senses and assignments of energy, our shaping perceptions of ourselves and our world. It is a lived
system of meanings and values. . . . [I]ts forms of domination and subordination correspond much more closely to the normal processes of social organization and control in developed societies than the more familiar
projections from the ideas of a ruling class (1977: 110).

Put another way, the exercise of power can be understood not
merely as imposed authority from the state through government,
but as mediated through cultural forms in everyday life and moral
imperatives—in society as a whole. Power is then internalized.

The social relations of production must be reproduced everywhere in society and its physical spaces. Hegemony is then understood as a relation of power embedded in a whole range of institutions, practices, social rules, and ideologies, some within the
specific apparatuses of the state and some in civil society. In civil
society, these relations, whether in the market, the family, the
community, art, or culture, appear as natural, politically neutral,
universal, self-evident, and commonsensical—part of everyday life

and economic activity. But they are not. It is precisely in the way that experience is taken for granted as common sense that defines hegemonic ideology and distinguishes it from propaganda or manipulation. The power of hegemonic ideology inheres in its capacity to organize the production of meaning and define how the world is understood: what exists, what is possible, what is good, cognitively and affectively (Therborn, 1980). But most important is the way in which the distinction between state and civil society disappears as the state includes all of the institutions within the social base of society—an expansion of politics beyond the boundaries of state bureaucracy.

Where does hegemony come from? Hegemony emerges from social formations and the struggles within them. The class structure, class power, and material arrangements that constitute capitalist society produce active social relations and practices based on the real ownership and control of production. Hegemony is therefore socially determined and not necessarily the product of political strategy. Class struggle, together with the social formation of capital as a whole, in its historical development, creates a hegemonic system, much as feudalism or monarchy creates its own order. In Marxian terms, it creates social consciousness. This consciousness, within and without the mode of production, produces a particular form of domination. While hegemony corresponds to some extent to the power relations derived from a capitalist social formation, it is not a simple reflection of that power but an ongoing feature of the entire social order, including the oppositional hegemony of the working class. In any case, the particular form hegemony takes cannot be predicted in advance since, as Chantal Mouffe explains, "it depends on a whole series of historical and national factors and also on the relation of forces existing at a particular moment in the struggle for hegemony. It is therefore by their articulation to a hegemonic principle that the ideological elements acquire their class character which is not intrinsic to them" (1979: 193). Hegemony is always in a state of change needing "to be renewed, recreated, defended, and modified" (Williams, 1977: 112). In advanced capitalism, the major hegemonic discourses include free markets, free exchange, contract, democracy, and individualism.

How does hegemony work in practice? How is it constituted?

Hegemony operates through various political practices and systems of meaning or historically constituted ideological frameworks which derive from contradictions of capitalism. They reify experience and construct reality. Through ideology, ruling classes link politically their economic, moral, and intellectual objectives to create a collective will. In Stuart Hall's terms, such ideological apparatuses consist of "concepts, categories, imagery of thought and systems of representation which different classes deploy to make sense of, define, and render intelligible how society works" (1983: 59). However, there is no necessary relation between ideologies and the relations of production. Hegemonic ideologies and apparatuses are located everywhere in society, for example, in mass media, churches, unions, schools, political parties, and family life. Power in society is expressed at every level of culture, whether actively or passively. Although hegemonic ideologies do not necessarily directly express the values of the dominant class, they cannot be separated from that class (Poulantzas, 1968).

Ideology makes hegemony possible and creates its own material existence. It is embedded in material practices and cultural forms not spiritual elements (Althusser, 1971; Lefebvre, 1976). Ideological struggles are struggles over meaning and discourse. Hall further elaborates that a central question for understanding hegemonic ideology is how it limits oppositional thought and becomes internalized. One answer concerns the way both everyday experience *and* those relations not immediately visible (as are market relations) become distorted and concealed. Thus people are not tricked or manipulated; rather, in Hall's view, they have inadequate explanations of the social system. Ideology does not create false reality or false consciousness but only a false interpretation. Ideological domination blocks the meanings people create for themselves. Hegemony is therefore not ideological inculcation. According to Colin Sumner, "social reality . . . and the forms of social expression are founded within and limited by the mode of production and its corresponding cultural and political structures" (1979: 288). Ideology is produced by everyday experience in a capitalist social order. Ideological categories "position us and prescribe social identities, e.g., consumers" (Hall, 1983: 77). Most important, ideologies are not superstructures. They are part of the totality of the social formation that defines the organization of capitalism. "Ideologies structure the world but are also embodied in features of that world. . . . They are an integral and substantive element of all social practice" (Sumner, 1979: 278, 290).

The political, economic, and ideological cannot be separated or understood as one causing the other in a linear relationship. One must avoid a reductionist view which sees the economic base as determining "in the last instance." Ideology does not directly express class interest nor can it be reduced to class interest. Ideological relations operate with some degree of autonomy in what Louis Althusser refers to as a structured totality (1971). The class/economic structure does not necessarily or automatically create ideologies congruent with the nature of its economic domination, even though ideologies flow partially from class power.

Hegemony works in social processes that arise out of the structure of capitalist control and not just in ideological practices. A feature of capitalist production, the form that the productive process takes, for example, assembly lines, scientific management, or social service production, automatically creates a system of control stamped with the imprint of capitalist domination. Such control operates not only as a means by which the labor process is managed or community order is sustained, but creates a type of social existence, a type of person suited to the new conditions. But the division of labor itself is not enough to achieve domination. Methods of work and forms of political life are intertwined with a specific form of consciousness, a way of life. This is how practice becomes ideological practice—by embodying ways of being and rules of social life.

The success of capitalist class hegemony requires mobilized consent to the social order; it depends on a coherent world view which is never questioned and which results in the separation of workers from control of the means of production, while capital retains control of the surplus. The particular interests of capital are presented as the general interest of all. The conditions for hegemony require political and social alliances with other classes, creating a "historic bloc" of social forces through consent and ideological activity. That is, hegemony requires mobilizing the consent of the dominated classes through moral and intellectual leadership. Mediators are, in Gramscian terms, organic intellectuals who provide a type of leadership that connects them to disputants, deepening their commitment.

Hegemony also requires the destruction of the unity of the working class and its projects, as well as those of other subordinate classes. Thus, ruling classes must broaden their interests to include elements of the working class and other popular social forces to win their consent. A social class seeking hegemony cannot rely only on its own perceived class interests. The needs, aspirations, and demands of subordinate classes not directly related to production must be considered and accounted for. Hegemony must oppose counterhegemony. More than this, it requires commitment—an active connection to the social order rather than just passive acceptance. Finally, it requires the state in all of its coercive powers as a last resort: in Gramsci's terms "hegemony protected by the armour of coercion" (1971). Coercion and consent are part of the same practice. Total hegemony is never achieved in capitalist society. Because domination depends on consent, the working class can mobilize for their own self-organization (Gramsci, 1971; Buci-Glucksmann, 1982). People may come to expect a kind of order too. Once they consensually participate in the production process, they may want it to provide security; even those who resist demand a wage.

Hegemony can be said to be effective when no appeals or justifications are necessary to gain assent and commitment to the social order as a whole, and when only limited resources are required to maintain order—either police or social resources. Hegemony works when active legitimacy is not necessary. According to Mouffe, "a class is hegemonic when it has managed to articulate to its discourse the overwhelming majority of ideological elements characteristic of a given social formation, in particular the national-popular elements which allow it to become the class expressing the national interest" (1979: 195).

Thinking about effectiveness also helps to define the boundaries of hegemony. The use of direct force is one boundary but so are active appeals for regime support and conscious engineering or extraction of mass consent. When order is no longer collaborative, when order must be imposed as a project, we are outside the boundaries of hegemony.

Hegemony works when it does not appear to be hegemony, but the natural result of the relations of production. Numerous indications exist that the hegemonic forces in American society are in crisis—the call for planning, the appeal to tradition, and law and order are examples. What is new about the crisis concerns, first, its scope: planning occurs at the level of finance capital on a scale and in realms undreamed of before World War II. It is precisely the coordination required for such planning that generates problems of order in public and private spaces previously untouched. Second, the appeal to tradition, always in conflict with changing values, loses its force as disagreements arise about what constitute the appropriate traditions, particularly with increased levels of immigration. Finally, the concern for ending corruption in government, expressed by leaders of corporate capital, demonstrates the impossibility of governing without deep state involvement in the economy. There are always struggles over ideology: because people have autonomy, because labor resists and reinterprets meanings, and because hegemonic ideology must permeate all social life in order to reproduce the relations of production.

At any given moment, capitalist hegemony contains an essential contradiction that makes it unstable, similar to the contradiction of the state in general: hegemony must support accumulation while employing noncommodified strategies, nonclass–oriented objectives. This tension is compounded by the need to work from existing nonclass–oriented ideologies, rather than creating whole new ideologies. More generally, hegemonic relationships are unstable because historical circumstances are always changing—within the mode of production and in people's experience and interpretation of reality.

NDR contains elements of direct repression and hegemonic ideology. Rooted in symbols associated with local culture, NDR creates a way of being in the world, a type of thinking, inconsistent with people's ordinary understanding and yet so seductive in its appeals that it becomes established in communities. It has direct connections to the state through the courts and local government (the armour of coercion), while creating an ambience of the everyday in its method and discourse of dispute resolution. NDR is hegemonic in the way its procedures create a consciousness that parallels the normal, self-evident understandings of everyday social organization. It blurs the distinction between state and civil society. The seemingly open-ended quality of its practices, typi-fied by the appearance of free flowing dialogue, and the give and take aspect of interactions among the participants, enhances its he-gemonic character. As people become immersed in mediation and committed to NDR's logic, the state's hegemony may be ex-tended. But there are many contradictions and hegemony is never permanent. It must be continually recreated. In order to grasp why and how the peculiar form of NDR occurs, we must explore, more generally, the ongoing crises in hegemony and the particular hegemonic crises emerging at this historical juncture.

THE CRISIS IN HEGEMONY

All capitalist hegemonies are unstable. No social order is self-producing; consent must always be constructed. In an expansion-ist economy such as capitalism, the construction of consent is both ambiguous and fragile. Under certain conditions, counterhege-monies arise to resist them. Hegemonic crises are failures of the political institutions and ideologies that reproduce specific social relations. A crisis exists when discourse in the public sphere lacks relevance to peoples' lives: when ideology is divorced from real life experience. Even though a consensus of sorts may be present, the consensus is less relevant because the language of rationality and authority appears arbitrary. People may endorse ideologies of the market, nuclear families, or communities, but these ideologies contain no integrating force. Counterideologies may then arise. Ideology gets abstracted from everyday experience. The disinte-gration of hegemony is found not in the breakdown of ideology but in its connection to everyday life. The crisis occurs within a context of the disintegrating social relations of production—not social values or order in general. The general crisis of hegemony is not a crisis in alienation, social disintegration, or disruption. Nor is it an economic crisis based on the falling rate of profit. Rather, it concerns the limits on the capacity to integrate people to prevailing cultural symbols and belief systems. The working class cannot be effectively integrated to the order of capitalism. Historical conditions such as the globalization of capital, because this further breaks the boundaries within which workers identify themselves nationally and establish their praxis, expand the contradictions of hegemony, creating a crisis in authority, identity, and the rationalization of conflict.

The crisis in hegemony, a permanent feature of capitalism, concerns the failure to contain counterideologies: to deny the form of human association and interpretation that derive from collective social experience. The crisis further involves the inability to minimize peoples' capacity to organize around social needs that oppose the logics of capital and to establish social and cultural forms independent of capital. People constantly recreate the conditions of their existence and reinterpret experience so that hegemony can never be finally reproduced or taken for granted. "The dominant culture . . . at once produces and limits its own forms of counterculture (Williams, 1977: 114). Moreover, the element of subjectivity (intentionality) remains. No authority or ideology can fully destroy imagination, irrational desire, or indeed the multitude of interpretations possible about what exists or what is possible, including how society should be constituted. People are themselves active agents, first connected to cultures, knowledge, and ways of understanding the world apart from capitalist logic. Endless struggles occur over meaning in everyday life and no ideology can eliminate the contradictions which give rise to them. Hegemony is always situational and the outcomes of struggle are contingent. The possibility for ideological reconstruction is always present. But there is something new about this crisis in the advanced stage of capitalism, particularly since World War II. In general terms, social reproduction in this stage, as noted, involves more than fragmenting political challenge or creating social stability. It requires active commitment and energy to its goals, not merely through passive acceptance of its ideological underpinnings but in the interactions that flow from them. Cooperation and consensus are crucial, but no one ideological framework can achieve these ends.

Because capital now operates within a global, integrated system, its infrastructure is a collectivity. That is, the institutions, space, time, movements, and human interactions within a given locale must be managed as a tightly knit structure, thoroughly implicated in production and consumption. Disruption to any one of the interdependent components affects the whole. The same

problems created for the state in managing an increasingly socialized labor force limit hegemonic ideologies. Why? The management of social life in its broadest sense throughout civil society
requires noncommodified, nontechnocratic ideologies only tan-
gentially connected to accumulation.

In many instances, the ideologies that integrate people to the
social order must oppose instrumental accumulation rationalities.
There is always a contradiction between the rationalization or instrumental reason necessary for capital expansion and the cultural
forms of everyday life which generate different social rhythms and
oppose technocratic logics. Capitalist rationality undermines all other
systems of meaning. As more relationships become commodified,
commercialized, and quantified, then work, productive activity,
culture, and social life become separated from a sense of purpose.
But as capitalism develops it weakens and bursts asunder those
institutions that traditionally provided both the framework for
stability and hegemonic values and symbols. Hegemony, because
it involves the construction of political subjects, is made more difficult as its social bases are eroded. Without a real social base
(community, family ties), hegemonic ideologies become incoherent. Just as socialists cannot rely on the unity of one working class
based purely on a concept of class, so capital cannot constitute a
unified subject through the commodity form or the artificial mass
cultural forms it creates (Laclau, 1983: 118–119).

The pace of disintegration of traditional culture and cultural
symbols has accelerated and disorganizes society at the micro level—
neighborhood, the family, and civic institutions—in new ways.
The family, for example, is not merely a place of support and
socialization. It becomes implicated in social regulation—an extension of state logics (Donzelot, 1979). At the same time, the symbols and rhetoric of community continue without the material reality
of the social life that produced them. These developments and the
homogenization of culture weaken the capacity to create new ideologies that can sustain connections to the social order. If existing
discourses have no relation to experience, rooting ideology in
working-class culture fails, especially as the economy declines. In
the public realm, in addition, the commitment to liberal democratic institutions, once considered the fundamental condition for
its political survival, inevitably deteriorates. This deterioration re-

sults from many forces, one of which concerns the impediment democracy produces to quick, unchallenged decision making. Capital's quest is for an apolitical society, conflict free, freed from time consuming procedures and debate. Thus democratic forms are sometimes purposefully eroded.

In increasing its own direct political influence, however, capital also limits the capacities of the state to manage conflict. As political parties, unions, neighborhood organizations, and other democratic institutions decline, the social order is left with forms of unmediated opposition, some of which will be absorbed in other state-administrative forms and some of which will produce confrontational politics.

Equally important, the rhetoric of democracy, even though it remains formalistic from the start, loses its ideological force as a means of legitimation and social integration. In Claus Offe's view, "politics as the struggle over substantive issues and politics as the institutional form of conflict resolution degenerates into informal and mutually disconnected modes of struggle and decision" (1984: 170). The breakdown between state and citizen at this level produces new social relations, characterized by further bureaucratization and less locally based organizational forms channeled through party apparatuses.

The weakened state is not prepared to handle new forms of political conflict that cannot be channeled through existing apparatuses because such concerns as ecology, feminism, or war and peace, are not based on conventional issues of distributive justice and involve different forms of consciousness. These issues concern ideologies, logics, and goals constituted by new political subjects outside traditional political discourses. They represent forms of expression not in accord with rationalistic discourse and therefore cannot be contained within rationalizing state institutional forms. The struggle over racial and sexual issues, Stanley Aronowitz explains, "challenges the social, economic, or ideological reproduction of society, either because it makes problematic capital accumulation processes or erodes the legitimacy of institutions that embody normative structures necessary for social and cultural domination" (1981: 106). The creation of new organizations emanating from the working class constitutes the basis for counter-hegemony—what Gramsci referred to as the war of position. Just as the formal state fails through external controls, hegemony, a characteristic of which is its internalization of control, weakens. Without the formal state apparatuses, more internal, self-imposed controls are necessary. And as the formal state apparatuses become more disconnected, unresponsive, and centralized, social conflict occurs in realms beyond their capacities. The exhaustion of the formal state (Wolfe, 1977) in ideological and resource terms and active efforts to eliminate its nonpolicing apparatuses, lead to an expansion of the informal state—a less structured form of the state which does not appear to be the state. This informalism occurs, not simply as a way of obscuring state power, but because of the flexibility it offers in an increasingly unpredictable social environment, resulting from capital expansion itself.

We have already described how labor is an infrastructure which must be managed as a collectivity, and how interpersonal conflicts can occur as a form of disruption. But we also need to understand conflict in everyday experience as a form of resistance in itself—in a way that could potentially be managed by more informal methods.

Disruption in capitalism is not merely organized political action but includes the way in which lived experience challenges its reason and refuses its subordinations. A great threat to capitalist domination is the possibility that, as it destroys traditional social structures, people comprehend the irrelevance of its logic and refuse to provide loyalty—a refusal that could lead to a more direct, conscious challenge with political purpose.

Specialized-rationalized thought never wholly masters or absorbs the raw material it subjugates. Labor power, nature, the body, the unconscious, speech—these raw materials maintain their nonidentity, difference, heterogeneity with respect to even the most thoroughly rationalized forms of science, morality, and aesthetics, and therefore remain points of origination for political struggles in the modern world (Brenkman, 1983: 23).

Class struggle involves conflict over practices and meanings as people experience them. Which conflicts will lead to an unraveling of hegemonic ideology can never be determined in advance, because there is no direct connection between the specifically capitalist logics and any particular cultural arrangement that exists along side it. Capital absolutely requires the subordination of a labor class and must cope with the cultural and political forms that emerge from everyday life. There is no way to predict what kind of social life is most suitable from capital's viewpoint. On the other hand, labor does not need capital. "The working class," Paul Willis reminds us, "is the only group in capitalism that does not have to believe in capitalist legitimations as a condition of its own survival" (1977: 123). Moreover, people create their own culture, if not just as they please. Although people's relationship to the means of production is partly structured and partly determined by their experience of it (not merely by what happens to them), this relationship is not received. "Social agents are not passive bearers of ideology but active appropriators who reproduce existing structures only through struggle, contestation, and a penetration of those structures" (Willis, 1977: 175).

No matter how tied to cultural practices, capital cannot fully contain the interpretation of experience—the conditions in which people find themselves—and therefore the control of such practices that emerge from everyday life. Cultural practices are always unpredictable and sometimes incompatible with capitalist imperatives. It is these practices that create a major aspect of hegemonic crisis and which complement the crises in specific ideologies directly tied to capitalist accumulation objectives.

The myths and symbols of capitalist society further generate desire beyond any hope of satisfaction. Precisely at a time when capital faces limits in its ideological focus on consumption, it reverts to an expansion of its cost-benefit, technocratic ideologies of commodification, the law of exchange, and bureaucratization, suppressing the reality of need. This creates a potential for cultural practices to become oppositional: to fail to reproduce or actively to undermine the social relations of production. Examples of oppositional ideologies in this regard include the refusal to work (Aronowitz, 1985), the refusal to achieve (Willis, 1977), and the refusal to learn (Bowles and Gintis, 1976).

Perhaps the most uncontrollable element of all is the desire for autonomy and control at work and in the community (Aronowitz, 1981). These counterhegemonies to capitalist logic derive from people's own rhythms, discourses, and interactions. They cannot be fully subordinated. They may or may not retain a class char-

acter or result in countermobilizations. To the extent that cultural
domination is eroded—either because it cannot address spiritual
needs or because it is discontinous with the interpretation of experience—there is a hegemonic crisis. Mass consumption/culture
cannot replace or redirect the desire for human interaction of a
certain kind without severe disruptions.

All of these crises, and the political struggles they produce,
transform the state and the way people are constituted as subjects
of the state. The legal relation, to which we now turn, is a major
form in which people are constituted within society.

CHAPTER 4

The Legal Crisis of the State

Neighborhood dispute resolution forums are not only forms of the state. They are organizationally situated within the judicial system. Therefore a brief examination of juridical relations in capitalist society and the impasses they pose for social reproduction is a preliminary step in explaining how informal mediation occurs as an option to the impasse.

Legal relations, as an element of state power, are embedded in reproducing the social order of capitalism and cannot be understood fully apart from this element. Law embodies and articulates class relations (Marx [1867] 1967; Pashukanis, 1978; Linebaugh, 1976; Hay et al., 1975; Poulantzas, 1978; Jessop, 1980; Cain and Hunt, 1979). It operates as an ideological form of class domination and an expression of state power that organizes property relations, production, contract, exchange, and relations between individuals. Legal categories often conceal the way in which the social relations of production and exchange determine entitlements. The assertion of class power is accomplished, in part by real power and influence over what is adjudicated and, equally important, by ideology. A central ideological feature is the differentiation between individual, civil, or citizen rights and collective rights associated with need whereby people are understood as members of social classes (Fraser, 1978; Neumann, 1957).

Law transforms economic power into a legal relation and class conflict into legal conflict, similar to the way in which social relations become commodity relations under capitalism.

So far as the commodity structure penetrates society in all its aspects and remoulds it in its own image so the juridical relation obtaining between separate and abstract, right and duty bearing subjects, expresses that economic relation in all its aspects either through legal institutions such as property and contract, or through what may be termed positive morality (Kinsey, 1978: 217).

The basic idea of free individuals establishing contracts with capital helps to support or sustain the fundamental capitalist prerogative of separating workers (producers of value) from ownership and control of the means of production.

But of course law does not and cannot merely regulate social and economic relations in the interests of capital, although capital's power is well reflected. Law does not "function" for capital, and its origins go beyond economic class conflict, emerging from political and cultural struggles. Thus, one cannot impute legal relations from the social relations of production. Legal hegemony is not automatic. It must be perpetually and actively constructed and requires consent among numerous classes and class fractions (Gramsci 1971; Sumner, 1979). Law must also be universal and partially autonomous from ruling class interests and the state apparatus in order that it appear to operate equally for all, presenting a (false) unity of interests between the classes—presenting the demands and aspirations of all classes. The "relative autonomy" of law and its mediating role make it an arena for struggle. No guarantee exists that it will reproduce capitalist social relations. Law educates and conditions the population, indirectly, about the political values of the dominant class and generates conformity to those values by conferring rights and rewards to subordinate classes. But it must do this by imposing a common code or language that defines rights of ownership and control.

To the extent that this code of legal principles is undermined or separated from universal ideals of justice, the legitimacy of legal principles, and the property entitlements they support, is placed in question. Yet capital itself is sometimes forced to undermine formal legality (the rule of law) and act in conjunction with purposive ends of the state. Although capital requires predictability achievable through formal procedures, it must also be able to disorganize and reorganize economic relations in order to meet the

demands for innovation in the social relations of production necessary for capital expansion (Hirsch, 1978; Hirschhorn, 1978). Such
innovation is often impeded by universal norms, fixed legal rules,
and procedures which stress the generality of law. For example,
efforts to manage inflation and recession, shift from coal to nuclear energy, prevent strikes, or conclude mergers are impeded by
health and safety regulations, antipollution laws, antitrust laws, or
the requirements of due process. Thus, the strains that develop in
judicial institutions parallel the inadequacies in other mediating institutions described earlier in this chapter. In more general terms,
formal judicial forms constrain the capacity to coordinate accumulation. As Charles W. Grau explains, summarizing Andrew
Fraser:

in the contemporary state concepts drawn from contract, property, and
tort law become irrelevant—the small scale commodity productions upon
which they are based have disappeared. The advent of overt economic
planning in the neocapitalist economy . . . requires increased cooperation
and coordination, giving rise to legal forms defined by status rather than
contract (1982: 198).

But capital is not alone in using the courts to pursue substantive
ends. Workers do so too. In the process they may create oppositional ideologies about law. They demand rights to a safe and
healthy work environment, full employment, and control over their
pension funds. Their efforts may undermine the foundations of
judicial authority and generate movement toward administrative
forms of justice (cf. Unger, 1975).

The assertion by labor of legal rights to employment or to a
safe and healthy workplace may threaten capital's rights of property and contract (Gintis, 1980). Capital cannot invest and move
as freely as it wishes; it cannot construct or locate productive facilities (e.g., nuclear power plants or factories producing dangerous chemicals), advertise certain products (e.g., children's break-
fast cereals), or produce given products (e.g., large, dangerous, or
polluting automobiles). Legal demands for the satisfaction of human needs—nutrition, health care, housing, clean air, and energy—may also reduce the control of capital over labor and its
share of the surplus value produced by labor. Conflict centers upon

material resources, public policy, market relations, and control of
everyday life rather than mere formal equality. The danger for
capital is not that property rights will necessarily be undermined—such a fundamental reordering of power cannot occur
through legal change alone. It is rather that extending the rights
of the laboring class obstructs capital expansion and hinders control over property solely through appeal to legal principle. As
Samuel Bowles and Herbert Gintis explain:

Capitalism structures practices through rights in property, to be exercised
by owners or their representatives, while liberal democracy vests rights
in persons. . . . These principles are in potential conflict. The principle
of free association of the workers is in direct opposition to the principle
of free individual contract (1982: 52).

Increasingly, more rights are being defined as person rights. In
the 1960s and 1970s expanded challenges to law occurred over
legal rights: constitutional rights, lawsuits challenging police authority, and demands for jury trials.

Legal rationality obstructs the ability of courts to manage new
forms of class conflict and economic dislocation arising from the
irrationalities of capitalist production. The problems posed by nuclear waste or genetic engineering cannot be resolved within the
narrow framework of technical legal rulings. These types of highly
volatile conflicts, particularly as they occur in community con-
texts, have not and possibly cannot be satisfactorily institutionalized within a judicial framework. More particularistic regulation
is required. Donald B. Strauss, former president of the American
Arbitration Association, is unwittingly revealing on this point.

With social disputes, there's usually no contractual relationship between
the parties. . . . In business you know who the parties in the dispute are
and what the basic issues are. Often that's unclear in community conflicts. . . . Perhaps the hardest problem is that you're not dealing with a
battery of high-powered lawyers and negotiators; you're dealing with activists who are not coldly logical (Ford Foundation, 1978b: 5).

The frustration with the unpredictability and disorder of political
action is an impetus for consensus mechanisms generally and me-

diation particularly. On one level is a need to exclude cases. Limiting what is justiciable proves difficult, not only because courts *must* respond to certain grievances (e.g., affirmative action) but also because capital requires innovative judicial policies that regulate more aspects of the social environment—both personal and political. At another level, capital must preempt, prevent, and include: tasks not suited to formal rules and organization.

As capital concentrates and centralizes its power, other class forces also organize, attempting to achieve some of their goals through judicial action. However limited such collective action may be, this type of challenge can reveal the class character of the law. These struggles reshape the form and content of legal conflict— usually in ways that highlight the political content of issues.

Labor and marginal populations also demand state benefits, which may come to be viewed as rights. State expansion into more areas of private social life sparks new battles over the distribution of public resources. At the same time, the formal procedures necessary to legitimate state action contain the potential to justify the further expansion of those rights.

Dislocation, actual or threatened such as plant shutdowns, dangerous products, and unemployment, also stimulates demands for better protection from the unplanned character and irrationality of the capitalist economy through complex regulations of products and liability for damages to those who suffer capitalist "mistakes," as in the recall of automobiles, the shutting of nuclear plants, the banning of pesticides, and restitution for consumer overcharges. The number and scope of such demands have been growing. They threaten capitalist power because they challenge the prerogatives of capitalists to produce and invest as they please. One result is new forms of the state that share many of the characteristics found in neighborhood dispute resolution forums.

Apart from direct challenges, the rule of law within the judicial system poses other constraints on the capacities of courts to handle effectively matters that come before them (Davis et al., 1980; Heydebrand and Seron, 1981). The judicial system is organized to handle certain types of disputes deemed appropriate. But the definition of appropriate keeps changing. For example, so-called small-scale or minor disputes have either been rejected by courts as nonjusticiable or relegated to small claims courts, shifted to arbitration procedures, or placed in a lesser priority on the docket. Such disputes are often described by judicial officials as "junk cases." Increasingly these types of neighborhood disputes at the level of everyday life—in contrast to those that involve loss of money or which occur among people who can handle them on their own— are becoming more disruptive to the social order. They disrupt the infrastructural stability necessary for capital accumulation. As Wolf Heydebrand explains,

a decreased capacity for formal conflict resolution may actually increase the level of substantive conflict in the larger society. Thus, by dismissing cases or inducing settlements, courts may temporarily terminate conficts but not ultimately resolve them. Instead, disputes are forced back into an indeterminate situation, that is, into the arena of conflicting socio-economic forces which had generated the dispute in the first place (1979: 47).

As the economy sinks into deeper crisis, and as citizens use the courts to secure their rights under public programs (Gintis, 1980), the disputes of working-class people with the state and among themselves may proliferate. More is at stake for them. But these people are not socialized to the ways of the courts. Judicial procedures are designed for the middle and upper classes and their problems. Formal procedures and the rule of law cannot handle the particularisms brought into court by people who cannot deal with formalism. Because the court is limited by formal procedural rules, it cannot confront the roots of conflict. It cannot therefore manage with precision solutions external to legal logic, given the relations between capital expansion and social disruption which have been described. Preemptive political intervention is required, regardless of whether such disruption can be defined by specific legal offenses.

The courts are increasingly politicized. They are geared to the protection of government policy against numerous claimants (e.g., Social Security, Medicaid and affirmative action). Under those conditions they become surrogates of the state and therefore less visibly autonomous. Sometimes they must protect the working class in a time of rising entitlements and at other times they become more of a foe as the state reduces entitlements. However, this relation of claimants with the state creates a crisis of legitimacy. When courts are perceived as not resolving disputes but as protecting the state and sometimes capital (e.g., anti-trust, oil leasing decisions), dissatisfaction occurs and hegemony is undermined. People do not use courts to be treated as a social problem but in order to receive a hearing. Disorder can thus mean too many people using the courts and making claims against the state. Too much litigation from the point of view of capital is thereby a form of disorder.

Legal rules and procedures in many ways are part of the infrastructure of daily life and in that sense represent a form of hegemony. For example, people take the courts and its rules for granted, as an orderly part of their communities (Danet, 1980). But increasingly, the kinds of conflicts arising in communities are more disruptive than previously. As judicial institutions become more isolated, bureaucratic, divorced from everyday life, and separated from the communities they serve, law loses legitimacy. The distinction between its reified abstractions and the culture become visible, experienced. The administrative failures of law in its implementation heighten its vulnerability and claims to legitimacy (Gramsci, 1971).

The unending effort to increase the rate of accumulation has given impetus to judicial reforms that have freed capital investment from normal legal restrictions. At the same time, given resistance from labor, it changes the way capital defends its control over the surplus through direct political intervention.

The response to these impasses has resulted in a new articulation among the structural components of law, by which I mean the organization of compliance and persuasion, and the relation between the bureaucratic and rhetorical aspects of law. Boaventura de Sousa Santos, for example, stresses that legal rhetoric "based on the persuasion and the production of voluntary compliance through mobilization of the argumentative potential of socially accepted verbal and non-verbal sequences and artifacts" is now dominant—compared with bureaucracy or the use of or threat of force (1982: 252). NDR possesses this quality. Its central features stress voluntary persuasion, argument, practicality, and a vernacular language, devoid of threats. NDR's most compelling characteristics, and those elements by which it is sold to the public, emphasize its difference and distance from bureaucratic or legal realms.

Social regulation in mediation happens through a series of carefully planned stages which, in an unofficial friendly setting, conceals its power. Disputants mutually agree to behavioral change
in harmonious fashion.

Neighborhood dispute resolution forums emerge from the contradictions and struggles in the judicial system that we have been
describing. Ironically, when the courts implement alternative procedures within an existing judicial framework to handle new
problems a contradiction emerges between its revised interventionist, problem solving mission and conceptions about its proper
role in achieving justice. Heydebrand comments

By cooperating in plea-bargaining and other forms of "justice by consent," courts help to delegitimize the judicial process. . . . A decision
short of adjudication may generate new contradictions between the court's
claim to legitimacy and its capacity to fulfill that claim (1979: 48).

Before detailing how NDR relates to the impasses in these institutions, it is necessary to elaborate on, in general terms, the
forms of the state that are now arising.

CHAPTER 5

Emerging Forms of the State

INTRODUCTION

A fundamental characteristic of the capitalist state in regulating the reproduction of labor is its scope and depth. The state expands and intensifies its activities. There are two aspects of this expansion, each interpenetrating the other. The first can be referred to as surveillance and regulation (intervention). The second is referred to as depoliticization or cohesion (representation).

Why surveillance? The state can no longer merely establish conditions for accumulation or protect workers from dislocations of capitalism. Capital now so thoroughly destroys the traditional social basis of control and stability that greater, more intensive surveillance-regulation is necessary. All of society's physical structures, instruments of production, services, and labor are viewed as resources that must be actively organized to foster capital expansion and manage it on a national basis (Harvey, 1976; Hirschhorn, 1978; Spitzer, 1979b; O'Connor, 1981a).

Thus the logic of subsumption, in which capital presses all social institutions into its service either as ideological or economic apparatuses, forms the core of what may be termed managed capitalism, which extends from the labor process to society as a whole (Aronowitz, 1978: 139).

Andrew Fraser elaborates this point in relation to the legal order:

More "private" aspects of the individual's identity and experience become legally relevant. . . . Since all standards of rationality and value within the corporate state stem from the universalizing power of capital, the legal process, if it is to be effective, must insure that any parochial particularities that cannot be dissolved and reconstituted as an element within the global hegemony of capitalist social relations are not permitted to impede the free flow of the rational forces of technology, capital, and labor, upon which social process depends (1978: 172–73).

People become targets for state action not because they engage in legally or morally culpable behavior but because of the relationship of their behavior and attitudes to the labor process, and the order of the social infrastructure through which production and consumption occur. "The distinctions between work and learning and learning and work and non-work break down" (Block and Hirschhorn, 1979). The private lives of individuals become relevant to capital. Intervention must be organized on a permanent and ubiquitous basis, because almost everyone and everything represents social capital and the potential for creating disruption in an accumulation process that requires increasing coordination. Cynthia Cockburn notes how "reproducing capitalist relations is more and more a cultural affair. It means school, social work, electoral politics . . . " (1977: 57). The goal of regulation is to direct and prescribe human labor power rather than exclude and confine it (Spitzer, 1982). All aspects of family and cultural life are involved in capitalist accumulation (Spitzer, 1981).

In the workplace, the needs of monopoly capital to expand productivity and minimize the disruption of production—both direct disruption of the work process as well as worker autonomy that limit capitalist prerogatives and the smooth administration of accumulation—make everyone "the subject of management interference" (Braverman, 1974: 309). That disruption concerns both conscious actions by workers to achieve autonomy and benefits (e.g. strikes), as well as the unpredictability associated with managing the labor process (Burawoy, 1979). Innovations in technology (see Noble, 1978) extend management authority over the work process by giving managers "the capability to time study production and skilled workers 24 hours a day. . . . Every minute of the worker's time can be accounted for. . . . The foreman no longer decides to discipline the workers. He merely carries out the automatic decisions of the system" (Shaiken, 1979: 13). Monitoring is characterized not merely by detailed observation but also by extensive probing and evaluation. Employers seek simultaneously to limit the discretion of workers, expand productivity, and limit challenges to capitalist prerogatives. To achieve these objectives, capitalists intrude on the privacy of workers by identifying those traits and attitudes that render workers amenable to control, regardless of their ability to perform the job function adequately (Edwards, 1979). An increasing number of jobs require applicants to submit to psychological tests (e.g., the Minnesota Multi-Phasic Personality Inventory). Workers in some industries have been genetically screened to determine their susceptibility to certain diseases known to be associated with the tasks performed. Rather than reform the workplace, the capitalist transforms and invests in the worker, using a variety of social engineering techniques: training, job enrichment, and worker satisfaction programs designed to involve workers in their own regulation.

At the community level, where NDR is located, state expansion is also characterized by extensive scrutiny of private lives by means of informal, decentralized mechanisms, located outside formal institutional settings, and heavy reliance on professionals in psychology and education (Szasz, 1965; Kittrie, 1971; Hylton, 1981; Brady, 1981). Methods of discipline, deviance management, social service delivery, and intervention in family life generally appear to be more closely related to labor market and labor force conditions than to conceptions of morality or law (Platt, 1969; Rothman, 1971; Jankovic, 1977; Foucault, 1977; Scull, 1977; Donzelot, 1979). The modern state is therefore noted for its penetration of the psyches of individuals, as well as preventive activities in order to preempt dissent, disruption, and deviance.

State surveillance-regulation concerns more than control of individual behavior ex post facto. As Claus Offe reminds us, the state creates more direct connections with individuals, even as the formal institutions and politics wither. The state mobilizes and manages human capital and resources, for example, education, health, and population policy. People are governed by more detailed regulation and, at the same time, their capacities are "developed, shaped, distributed, and allocated by specific state policies" (Offe, 1984: 175).

The expanded state which polices and conditions is not merely

a welfare or a police state but a hegemonic state seeking to constitute society. Thus, the second aspect of the expanded state is
depoliticization–cohesion which concerns the means of representation more than it does intervention, even though they overlap.
While the surveillance mode seeks to include, intrude, and supervise, depoliticization emphasizes excluding people from decision
making and fragmenting their capacities for mobilization. More
than this, the state must generate consent to the social order. Such
consent means two things. It involves a process of demobilizing
political activity, that is, inhibiting the possibility of alternative,
oppositional, collective approaches to social order. This is its passive aspect. At the same time, and in a more activist role, the state
in advanced American capitalism demands commitment to the
agenda of capital expansion and the ideologies that sustain it.

   In seeking to realize these subobjectives of surveillance and depoliticization, the state takes on new forms. The two most pre-
dominant forms can be referred to as planning and informalism or
the informal state. Each bears a relationship to and, in some ways,
contradicts the other. Their emergence suggests a more activist,
interdependent state concerned with greater precision in reproducing the relations of production. More than that, each represents
the nationalization of the social order and the decline of politics.
They constitute basic structural characteristics which define NDR.

PLANNING

   Planning within a capitalist framework is the rationalization of
social life in order to expand capital accumulation and reproduce
the labor force. It is a form of institutionalized collective action
and occurs at the level of capitalist society as a whole, whereby
capital becomes more cosmopolitan, less accountable, and less
connected to the local level (see Sklar, 1980). More areas of social
life become coordinated objects of public policy (e.g., energy, education, transportation, interest rates), particularly as capital becomes more concentrated, centralized, and interdependent. In essence, planning is a form of social management and nondemocratic
decision making that centralizes power and decentralizes function,
replacing democratic institutions, public involvement, and public
debate with administrative institutions.

Planning also involves cooperation and consensus at the top, in order to achieve coordination without democratic or even public processes. It is therefore an example of the "informal state" at the upper levels of the state. "The consensus that underlies major state policies is a consensus that does not result from a democratic process . . . but a consensus resulting from informal, highly accessible negotiations among poorly legitimized representatives of functional groups" (Offe, 1984: 167–68).

These planning arrangements, in contrast with political parties and the rule of law, structure and channel economic and social activities that potentially produce disorder for capital (Habermas, 1975). Thus, planning means greater authoritarian control, both in a technical and political or class sense. Control is partially administered by the capitalist class itself, so that the state becomes an administrative servant—not an executive committee—of the capitalist class.

Planning represents a response to economic instability, the failure of political processes, limits on the ability of individual capitals to generate needed investment, regulate business cycles, and subsidize social costs of production, and certain problems in the crisis of the state: the need for responsiveness to a single center, to make sources of control clearer and more routine, to reduce "wasteful" competition, to create macroorganizational coordination, and to deal with the political constraints set by liberal democracy.

Conscious efforts to plan, which began in the Progressive era, have been a major element of capitalist social control since the New Deal, launched in response to the centralization and concentration of capital and the failure of markets to marshall and allocate resources. Planning arises because neither markets arranged around price, profit, competition, and politics, nor formal decision structures such as law or local government, can guarantee the conditions for accumulation, the reproduction of the labor force, and the social relations of production (Hirsch, 1978). Capital cannot provide the preconditions for its own existence because of the increasing socialization of production. That is, the control of noncapitalist, noncommodity existence requires decision making that conflicts with ordinary commodity logic and market criteria. Planning seeks to deal with the anarchy of the situation, not only

through centralized management but with the application of scientific criteria and organizational logic. Now, as then, planning
aims to reduce uncertainty about the supply of labor, resources,
and financing; to create investment opportunities; to control prices,
costs, and demand; and otherwise to limit impediments to accumulation and manage the extraction and realization of surplus value.
Planning is thus capital's method for organizing its environments.
It is "a historically-specific and socially necessary response to the
self-disorganizing tendencies of privatized capitalist social and
property relations as these appear in urban space" (Dear and Scott,
1981: 13).

Contemporary planning is distinguished by two features: first,
it supports capital as a whole, rather than individual industries or
some fraction of capital; second, it increases the centralization of
decision-making authority while decentralizing function and deprives workers and democratically elected officials of control over
basic aspects of economic and social life. It therefore represents a
major change in the organization and scope of the state. Planning
also occurs in relation to insurgency and instability in city politics.
The idea of the corporate state embodies the central theme of
planning—above political institutions, insulated from democratic
political control. Planning, above all, replaces democratic politics
by establishing institutions that manage the social order and by
reducing the focus of challenge through local politics. The opportunity then arises for tighter control over the work force.

A key element of planning is administrative-technocratic rationality (Habermas, 1975; Heydebrand, 1979). This is a form of social interaction that mediates class conflict by transforming the organization and language of political challenge so as to conceal class
interests and fragment the collective power of labor. Public policy
is translated into questions of science. This depoliticization of conflict is partly realized by replacing explicitly political and democratic decision-making structures with administrative institutions
and procedures dominated by experts unaccountable to the public.
The collective power of labor is disorganized, artificially separating public and private interests (citizens versus persons), regulating people by relegating them to limited roles (workers, patients,
clients, disputants, etc.), and, more generally, transforming class

relations into relations between and among individuals, groups, or abstract entities.

During the 1970s, corporate executives and former public officials created the Trilateral Commission, the Business Roundtable, and the National Industrial Conference Board, along with other political action committees, trade associations, and planning agencies to generate capital and extend capitalist control by garnering state subsidies, reorienting educational institutions toward specific policy goals, increasing the power of the executive branch of government, and reducing popular challenges to established authority by limiting the growth of democratic institutions and any expansion in the entitlements of the working class (Sklar, 1980).

The call for economic planning has expanded as the economy has begun to deteriorate sharply in the 1980s. Corporate liberals, corporate leaders, economists, and even some conservatives advocate the creation of national industrial policy to moderate the so-called imperfections of markets and establish priorities in allocating resources, although they differ on how to do it and which industries to support (see Reich, 1982; Heilbroner, 1978; Thurow, 1980). Felix Rohatyn, the investment banker, supports a Reconstruction Finance Corporation (RFC) that would coordinate investment on a national basis by providing capital in return for some degree of control over management and concessions from labor.

The RFC should provide the kind of capital our older industries sorely lack: equity capital. . . . Only an RFC that is publicly accountable but is run *outside of politics* [emphasis added] . . . could provide such capital as well as negotiate the often stringent concessions that have to come with it (1981: 19).

Ira Magaziner and Robert Reich (1982) also support the idea of public investment banks and targeting specific industries that promise economic growth. Harvard economist Wassily Leontief contends that our economy operates without a long-run perspective. He has argued for "systematic coordination of investment based on long-range foresight. That is planning" (1982: 32, 33). What many recent planning schemes share is a means by which the state will subsidize certain investments (education, housing) and reduce taxes, while still appropriating profits privately. The objectives are "not to [aid] the poor or [protect] the natural environment, but to [subsidize] the private expansionary process" (Connelly, 1981: 12).

More specifically, we can examine manifestations of planning in the workplace, the community, and the judicial system. In the workplace, planning takes the form of comprehensive research into and coordination of long-range production needs. Control is centralized to enhance managerial authority and remove decision-making authority from workers (Braverman, 1974). Limiting the autonomy of workers to plan and execute work is necessary for innovation. Control can also be separated from the geographic location of work. The corporation can thus separate itself from a local base or constituency and mobilize a labor force to suit specific production needs, while simultaneously dispersing the concentration of working populations that may produce disruption. Moreover, technocratic authority in the form of rules replaces individual discretion in the supervision of work, concealing employer control. Workers thus struggle over compliance with rules but not over their content or source.

Work activities become defined and directed by a set of work criteria . . . rules, procedures, and expectations . . . [and] formalized job descriptions . . . [rather] than by specific orders, directions, and whims of the supervisor. . . . From these criteria derive the "customary law" notions of "equity" or "just cause" in firing, promotion, and assignment. . . . Top echelon management . . . set the criteria, establish the structure, and enforce compliance. . . . Power thus becomes institutionalized by vesting it in official positions or roles and permitting its excercise only according to prescribed rules, procedures, and expectations (Edwards, 1978; 119, 120).

By structuring every detail of the work process through the classification of each job title, task, or procedure and establishing incentives for meeting specifically defined criteria, management encourages workers to

pursue their self-interest in a narrow way as individuals, and [stifle their] impulse to struggle collectively for those same self-interests. . . . The ability to establish rules provided the capitalists with the power . . . to set the basic conditions around which the struggle was to be fought. . . . As workers were isolated from each other, and as the system was made distinct from the bosses who supervise it, the basic capitalist-worker relation tended to shrink from sight (Edwards, 1979: 145–46).

Administrative criteria also transform the worker and the workers' needs into abstract categories measured according to scientific methods and cost-benefit theory. The capitalist desires to

translate the emotional language of life and limb into the more dispassionate and measurable idiom of cost accounting. . . . What exactly is health "worth"? How does one reasonably trade off profit against safety? Even the most sophisticated methods produce logical absurdities that violate commonsense ideas of justice and equity (Green and Waitzman, 1980: 42).

Workers lose control over grievances on the shop floor when professional experts such as third-party mediators or arbitrators clarify norms in advance and decide the outcomes. Workers rely on the union, management, and even government to translate conflicts into acceptable terms (Aronowitz, 1973; Stone, 1981; Klare, 1982). Agreements rarely deal with daily grievances or the changing conditions in the workplace that accompany the constant reorganization of the work process. Workers usually lack a grievance mechanism that is free of management control.

In handling specific grievances on and off the shop floor, as well as major eruptions such as strikes, conflict resolution procedures are usually established in advance by the capitalist. The process adheres to fixed criteria in a regular, complex, and codified system with limited appeals. Many labor contracts, for example, specify arbitration as the primary tool of dispute resolution in order to guarantee labor peace and reduce labor costs. But arbitration accepts the basic discrepancy in power between capital and labor and reduces struggle to routine administrative formulas. Although negotiation and arbitration are not new, they have now been applied more thoroughly to all realms of industrial conflict, including shop floor grievances. At a broader level of policy, capital plans the relocation of plants, not merely to seek the greatest return on cap-

ital per se but to disrupt unity and choose regions where union
activity is weak (Bluestone and Harrison, 1980).

The application of planning criteria to the organization of work
parallels developments in community politics and in struggles over
the distribution of resources, investment, and public policy. Urban planning is a form of state social control, reinforcing rationalizing tendencies to manage consumption, labor, markets, and
land use, as well as a means for the capitalist class to legitimate
itself. More specifically, urban planning rationalizes or commodi-
fies the uses of urban space, the consequences of uneven development, and responds to underinvestment, waste, and the ungov-
ernability of the city in capital's interests (Mollenkopf, 1977). City
life is chaotic and anarchic and cannot be governed by market
criteria and individual initiative (Cox, 1981).

When the dislocations, irrationalities, and conflicts of the urban system
began to subvert prevailing social relationships, urban planning makes its
appearance as a means of collectively readjusting the spatial and temporal
developments of urban land use (Dear and Scott, 1981: 13).

Planning is designed to deal with the management of space and
the production of the infrastructure (transportation, housing, employment policy, and public facilities, etc.) necessary for continued accumulation and the reproduction of labor (Cockburn, 1977;
Harvey, 1981: 103).

Urban planning essentially replaces both traditional political institutions of local government and politics itself by establishing
corporate administrative forms that can act decisively and quickly.
These forms replace advocacy and challenge and support capital's
capacity to control local politics at the same time as they seek
freedom from political control by local government. "Metropolitan planning arrangements will help to obviate local controversy
by screening local decisions from public scrutiny. . . . [T]he ob-
scurity is deepened by the technical and scientific procedures which
are a natural corollary to the emphasis on planning" (Piven and
Cloward, 1972: 248). Thus, planning is also a type of political
organization and decision making that occurs partially above the
political system, designed to create the ensemble of material conditions that will secure a social order compatible with accumula-

tion. From the viewpoint of planners, planning also deals with system "overload," not only in relation to political demands but also with respect to the intensification of land use and congestion.

The roots of urban planning can be traced to Progressive era reforms, such as city manager government and nonpartisan, at-large elections, which were designed to limit the threat that democratic rule posed to the authority of capital (Hofstadter, 1955; Weinstein, 1968). Prime examples of contemporary planning are the creation of regional planning bodies, run by expert administrators, who design urban renewal, transportation, and sewer projects and whole cities in conjunction with real estate interests and banks (Piven, 1972). Perhaps the most extraordinary instance of planning in recent years occurred in 1975, when New York City created the Emergency Financial Control Board, which effectively undermined the authority of elected city officials by giving finance capital the power "to review revenue and expenditure estimates and to monitor the budget, and . . . overrule municipal union contracts freely negotiated" (Newfield and Dubrul, 1977: 179). Metropolitan governments, encompassing parts of several states, are another response to problems posed by fragmented local governments that restrict the capacity of capital to dominate a city because no single authority can develop a comprehensive policy to encourage capital investment and restrict the claims of labor and surplus populations.

An example of urban planning with a direct relation to informal mediation and corporatism is the Negotiated Investment Strategy (Committee for Economic Development, 1980). This is a technique devised by the Kettering Foundation, the Committee on Economic Development, and urban planners to direct municipal investment policy. It seeks to demonstrate that "labor-style negotiation can overcome the competition and poor coordination among government agencies that have long confounded urban planning" (Herbers, 1979: 1).

At the level of the individual, centralized planning means that the objects of control are increasingly responsive to more coordinated control. Instead of John Doe the worker, the consumer, the student, with different institutions responding to different institutional roles, all three may be regulated together at the level of everyday life (Esland, 1980). Family life, for example, is increasingly regulated by public agencies that interact with one another (Donzelot, 1979). Officials make decisions—about services and budgets—according to administrative criteria and managerial efficiency, in processes insulated from politics.

Two aspects of planning differentiate the last two decades. The first is quantitative in character: the application of planning to more areas of social life and public policy. Democratic decision making is further removed from the community, first by limiting public participation to perfunctory attendance at hearings or memberships on boards or commissions with minimal authority. The second is qualitative: the creation of permanent planning agencies and the integration of funding agencies.

However, there are limits to planning. Steven Spitzer identifies a number of countereffects:

the enormous costs and political problems created by the corrosive effects of capitalist development on traditional social institutions and modalities of informal control (the family, the church, community, etc.) . . . and other impediments to the leveling and atomization of subject populations for both economic and political purposes; the growing problems associated with the management of superfluous populations . . . the creation of new "pockets of resistance" to the rationalization process; special interest groups; . . . and [cutbacks] in "human services" [necessary to develop capitalism's productive forces] (1979b: 201).

In sum, what Spitzer suggests is that capitalist technocratic rationality confronts the rationality of everyday life and social struggle that resist such planning. Equally important, although community planning bodies such as neighborhood councils, established as a means to coopt community organization, cannot control major government decisions, they can challenge or otherwise delay decisions.

Moreover, as planning repoliticizes social relationships, it generates organized opposition because of its increased visibility. It legitimizes and encourages political activity over a widening range of subject matter. Planning activity also conflicts with efforts by capital to retain control over investment. As Offe explains, "capital can define the limits and boundaries of 'realistic' public planning. . . . State planning can only ever be partial and incomplete" (1984: 21).

Planning, as a characteristic application of technocratic or instrumental reason, further destroys the traditional bases of social control in society. In the effort to coordinate the system, planning undermines the source of hegemony. More than a problem of efficiency versus legitimacy, planning and planning rationality destroy the capacity for generating meaning which is essential to social control. Planning criteria are those of the law of value. Yet the form of administrative control subverts the commodity form (Offe, 1984).

Planning is more comprehensive in almost all aspects of production as capital becomes more concentrated and centralized. The expanded role of the state in planning the production process has important implications for the character of judicial institutions of social control. One implication is that this involvement, whether it means distributional changes through social services or expansion of civil rights, essentially constrains the extent to which capital can rely on labor markets to discipline labor. This expanded involvement in production and consumption locates struggle in the political process: an arena less amenable to direct capitalist control. The effectiveness of the state's interventionist capacities is limited not merely by fiscal constraints or even by revealed connections with class interests. Although the state handles numerous forms of dislocation, it cannot solve the central contradictions of a capitalist society in which the structure of capital accumulation is itself the barrier to greater expansion. As Joachim Hirsch explains:

When the decline in the rate of profit and the tempo of accumulation becomes manifest, this must lead to an intensified exploitation of labour power mediated through the state apparatus, while at the same time potential state resources for "superfluous" measures of pacification and reform—"superfluous," that is, for the immediate profit interests of capitals—are drastically restricted. This is the context in which the "consequences" of economic growth—decay of the cities, chaotic traffic situation, collapse of the ecological equilibrium, etc.—become politically explosive: not because the "managing capacity" of the state is too small in a technical sense . . . but because capital comes up against the self-produced barriers of its valorization, which can be broken through only by an intensification of exploitation and class struggle (1978: 105).

Although planning would seem a logical outgrowth of capital expansion in the realms described so far—the economy and urban environments—it is particularly striking to discover its forms within the judicial arena. On the surface, the application of principles of justice might seem to contradict the delivery of justice according to management principles.

For about the last eighty years, and most dramatically the last decade, the judicial system has been a subject for planning as a means for coordination with a variety of themes, all of which are associated with what Wolf Heydebrand would refer to as technocratic forms of administration (1979). The same problems of coordination, flexibility, efficiency, fiscal crisis, demands for access and services, and rationalizations that give rise to planning in other realms apply with equal force to the judicial system, although the effects are not uniform or unidirectional. Technocratic strategies can be seen to "[emerge] from the structural control needs of a system that seems largely out of control" (Heydebrand, 1979: 52). Similar principles of planning, derived initially from scientific management and administrative controls applied in the workplace and municipal government were applied to the organization of courts (Pound, 1940; Friesen et al., 1971; Harrington, 1982: 42, 45). Planning was a response to problems in coordination and management—the growing complexity, specialization of issues, inefficiencies, and lack of supervision, as well as problems of social control (Heydebrand and Seron, 1981; Harrington, 1982).

Extensive and permanent managerial planning of judicial institutions began in 1938 at the federal level with the "formation of the Administrative Office (of the Courts) and the Federal Judicial Center with responsibilities for monitoring, planning, and guiding the modernization of the courts" (Heydebrand and Seron, 1981: 412). Over the years, similar institutions at the state and local level have arisen with objectives directed toward the management of courts—for example the National Advisory Commission on Criminal Justice Standards and Goals, and the American Judicature Society.

During the 1970s, advocates for planning and systemic reform of the courts abounded (Rosenberg, 1972; Friesen et al., 1971; Early, 1972; Burger, 1976; National Center for State Courts, 1978). The National Judicial Planning Association was formed in 1978 for the purpose of improving "the administration of justice through planning" (Criminal Justice Newsletter, 1978). In 1979, the United States Department of Justice funded a major study "designed to meet some of the major needs which civil justice system planners will face in the 1980s" (Trubek, 1979: 1). The introduction of technical innovations such as data processing and forecasting are only the most recent efforts at rationalization in the judicial arena.

Federal planning of criminal justice began in earnest with the Omnibus Crime Control and Safe Streets Act of 1968 which created the Law Enforcement Assistance Administration (LEAA). By means of standards and goals, rules, programs, technologies, and exemplary projects, LEAA had, in its thirteen years of operation, significantly influenced the shape of criminal justice throughout the nation. It monitored, evaluated, and coordinated numerous dispute resolution programs. During the early 1970s, LEAA expanded its rationalization of control with planned systems of alternatives to conventional adjudication across the entire judical system (Aaronson et al., 1977).

The dialectical movement between centralization (of control) and decentralization (of function) has been a basic and continuing characteristic of planning since the Progressive era. One basic movement toward centralization can be identified in various proposals for court unification (Pound, 1940; Berkson and Carbon, 1978). Court unification refers to the consolidation of state appellate and trial courts into one system, thereby centralizing management through a chief judge who would organize caseloads and supervise personnel. Court unification at the local level was embodied in municipal court movements, its objective being to gain greater managerial supervision.

Informal dispute resolution, planned at the top but decentralized in function, represents an aspect of judicial planning in its historical association with many other of its elements, including the streamlining of procedures, the realization of order maintenance, the creation of specialized courts and judges, the use of experts, and flexibility. The tensions and constraints that generate planning of informal, decentralized processes can also be traced to the Progressive era (Harrington, 1982). Planning in this instance involved similar rationalizations and emphasized nonlegal aspects of social life in the particular institutions established, such as juvenile courts, domestic relations courts, and small claims courts. Much as planning bodies operate external to formal political processes, informal procedures, sometimes operating within conventional courts, were designed to handle conflict through a social process that was essentially nonlegal. These processes, however, were formally linked and that is what ties them to planning. They did not arise randomly. As we shall see, the central features of planning are found in the NDR centers. And their planning is related to problems in managing social life and social environments more deeply, as well as to constraints within the judicial system.

THE INFORMAL STATE

State power and the way it is used (the form of the state) is changing with respect to what were once peripheral areas of domination (Santos, 1982; Cohen, 1985). These areas of social life where the state did not need to go and where it had little effect—at the community level—now become more important. This is because, as we have explained, the community itself, its institutions and physical space, become implicated in production and reproduction. To the extent that the state penetrated the community in the past, it did so at the risk of losing legitimacy, through the use of obvious repressive forms of domination—such as the police and the bureaucracy. Now we witness the growth of institutions, such as neighborhood dispute resolution forums, which enter aspects of social life that have previously been of peripheral interest to the state but which cause disruption to capital expansion and the extraction of surplus value or become closely connected to production, consumption, and exchange relations, particularly in volatile urban environments.

Every society or social formation requires forms of social integration. But under capitalism, these forms, also embedded hegemonically in ordinary processes and rhythms of social life, may connect the populace to exploitive institutions while simultaneously concealing their authority. Informal processes in everyday life, normally thought of as governed by community norms to protect social order, are connected specifically if indirectly to capitalist imperatives and the peculiar requirements for order that are exploitive at their base. The informal state at the grassroots is a relatively new form of state power that represents its expansion into civil society but appears as a contraction of state power or remains unrecognized as the state. It is a return to purposive, flexible decision making which is instrumental, result-oriented, particularistic, and regulatory, without norms or standards, yet embedded in the cultural mode of everyday life. It uses social criteria instead of legal or moral criteria. It arises in the absence of organic communities or political solidarity.

The form of relations among people or groups is reorganized in such a way that domination is inherent in the form of the activity itself rather than external to it or embedded in norms. The informal state differs from external control, bureaucratic-hierarchical controls, planning, compliance, and overt cooptation mechanisms in that it is a form of hegemony. Informal control is obscured and operates in predetermined, accepted organizational forms and processes such as political parties and labor unions. It emerges from resistance to existing controls and supplements rather than replaces them in most instances. The informal state is a form of the state that appears as nonstate, employing ideologies and practices from everyday life.

The informal state further arises from the need to anchor people to the total social system of capitalist relations. It emerges in response to the state's efforts to create bonds with labor and the failures of welfare state programs. As Hirsch explains, "The capitalist state consists of numerous apparatuses that are not merely management oriented. [The state] must maintain links with the proletariat and with other classes and strata not to be counted as part of the bourgeoisie" (1978: 100). These informal modes develop not only because of the impasses previously described in traditional institutions of repressive state social control, but because capital must create alliances with fractions of labor if it is to succeed (Gramsci, 1971). Open class warfare is costly and creates resistance to accumulation and the realization of value that depend on acquiescence and affirmative support. To sustain growth and present its costs as a public interest is a general requirement of state control (Cox, 1981). J. A. Agnew explains how "following Marx, several writers have argued for the importance . . . of a practice of 'practical incorporation': the expansion of commitment to the prevalent social order by the development of personal stakes in its survival . . . " (1981: 457). Social integration is made difficult because it must also deal with the consequences of overrationalization and commodification that result from planning.

Capital expansion cannot proceed by rationalized efficiency techniques of its steering capacities alone (Habermas, 1975). It must be able to realize and not just produce its potential (Burawoy, 1979). At the same time, the conditions for innovation must be constantly recreated. These objectives cannot be fully achieved by force or obvious manipulations. The informal state, focusing on cooperation and participation, is difficult for opponents to attack directly.

What the informal state accomplishes when it works is an expansion in the capacity to neutralize and disorganize collective action and political expression by defusing, confining, displacing, and disarming discontent, fostering dependency on capital, and incorporating the working class and segments of surplus population. This must occur in such a way that accumulation is not challenged or disrupted while simultaneously reproducing class relations and maintaining the prerogatives of capitalist power. The objective is not overt repression or the elimination of conflict. Rather, it is to structure, channel, institutionalize, trivialize, and absorb it. The idea is both to create acceptance of authority that does not appear as authority (negative antagonism) and to create a basis for regulation, without the appearance of regulation.

The key to understanding the informal state lies in how it is instituted or embodied in institutions of everyday life in relation to a particular kind of order conducive to capital expansion. Such control is not entirely new and is essential to any society. But under capitalism informalism makes sense based on understanding the character of everyday life and the ways capitalist institutions and the capitalist mode of production permeate everyday life or are embodied in it. New forms of state control emerge in different historical periods. Earlier forms were connected to ideologies and language (Thompson, 1966; Spitzer, 1982). Contemporary forms are not connected so much to language as to managing activities of daily life, based on the detailed penetration of private life through the state, already discussed. New forms, such as neighborhood councils, neighborhood planning bodies, and neighborhood crime watch, are now applied to areas where external or bureaucratic control normally dominates. Or the forms are applied in traditional institutions such as police crisis intervention units and community mental health centers. At issue, then, is how informal control is achieved (or thwarted) in dividing the working class. These new forms, moreover, parallel those elements central to neighborhood dispute resolution.

What are the basic elements of the informal state? First, its method is to *involve* people in a process or activity that provides a sense of control. Fulfillment is derived from investing oneself in a process such as mediation. Active, voluntary, positive participation is contrasted with exclusion, compulsion, and cooptation. (Cooptation occurs when hierarchical institutions within the state seek support from the populace). People interpret their participation as an opportunity. The rules for participation come from above but are not understood as such. This form of involvement is in sharp contrast with other forms of involvement exemplified by social protest, boycotts, lobbying, civil disobedience, and lawsuits. Artificial forms of involvement created by the state are "based on a substitution of . . . commitment and courage for position and authority" (Perlman, 1978: 76). The potential effect harnesses people to the state in a dependent relationship and redirects attention and participation from civil, nonstate forms of social action. As involved participants, people are partly responsible and therefore less likely to challenge basic premises.

An important aspect of involvement is internalization, a process whereby domination is accepted as natural. "People often accept what exists as necessarily legitimate—not consciously as the result of moral reflection but unthinkingly as a result of continuous involvement in everyday life" (Agnew, 1981: 459). The internalization of categories and values of capitalist society is not new. However, the growing discontinuity between material experience during times of severe dislocations and received ideology influences the creation of processes which sustain images that do not conform to reality. They arise through the ordinary practice of everyday life and not an obvious, alien form of authority or rules which clearly derive from such authority. In short, control cannot appear as control in order to be effective. This is what potentially makes informalism hegemonic.

A second element concerns the use of the appearances of everyday life, both in the nature of interaction and discourse. At the level of interaction, the symbols of state authority are absent: no flags, badges, uniforms, or formal ritual. At the level of discourse, rhetoric and speech replace the language of bureaucracy and the rule of law (Santos, 1982). In addition, the emphasis on facts and objective conditions is supplemented with or replaced by the subjective, by consciousness: how one feels becomes more important than what happened. Problem solving and behavioral correction replace norms and rights. This individualization of interaction conceals the exploitive character of interaction defined by the capitalist mode of production.

Third, *consensus*, mutual interest, cooperation, understanding, and partnership are emphasized rather than antagonism or adversarial relations that arise out of power differentials. The identification of common (class) interests is encouraged in an atmosphere of compromise and conciliation. Informal state control is therefore a means of inclusion rather than exclusion (Spitzer, 1982).

A fourth element concerns the further transformation of the public sphere into the private sphere and social issues into interpersonal problems. While an important characteristic of capitalist society is the separation of the economic and political realm, the informal state limits the space of the public sphere. The emphasis on self-help, self-control, and voluntarism define some of this development. Representation is face-to-face and direct, further minimizing the perceived presence of the state. The consequence is a continued isolation and an emphasis on self-regulation or self-policing that replaces social change with stress management. The exploitive character of interaction within the capitalist mode of production may then be concealed through an image of popular sovereignty.

Two additional elements of the informal state concern its location in time and space. The informal state is preemptive, seeking in advance to identify areas of activity that might be disruptive, prior to any specific action or rule violation. In this sense, it is affirmative rather than reactive. Yet it appears to be spontaneous and responsive. Finally, the informal state at the local level (in contrast with planning) disperses control or decentralizes its function, so that control lacks formal boundaries (Foucault, 1977; Cohen, 1985; Spitzer, 1982). These elements are not mutually exclusive, nor do they necessarily operate in any fixed manner. The informal state is manifested in the workplace and the community.

In the workplace, informal control is embedded in the work process itself in the division of labor, as organized by the capitalists (see Braverman, 1974; Friedman, 1977; Pignon and Querzola, 1978; Burawoy, 1979). It is also a form of control exercised at the more general level of labor-management relations (Aronowitz, 1978; Klare, 1982).

Perhaps Michael Burawoy best characterizes the way in which consent in the workplace is dependent on participation in a process, irrespective of conscious interpretations.

Unlike legitimacy, which is a subjective state of mind . . . consent is expressed through, and is the result of, the organization of activities. It is to be distinguished from the specific consciousness or subjective attributes of the individual who engages in those activities. Within the labor process the basis of consent lies in the organization of activities as though they presented the worker with real choices, however narrowly confined those choices might be. It is participation in choosing that generates consent (1979: 27).

At the point of production, informal control is found in the organization of the work process through the division of labor. Such control is not new but takes new forms. A good example, quoted at length, is provided by Dominique Pignon and Jean Querzola in their discussion about the reorganization of work at the American Telephone and Telegraph Company.

[T]ake the example of the punch-card operators and checkers. The job of the employee is to mark on a punched card the customer's statement of account; . . . in New York alone 200,000 cards . . . are handled every day. Before the reforms . . . the women employees were divided into two groups of card-punchers and checkers . . . a supervisor divided the work out. . . . After some discussion . . . a modification was decided on. Instead of being divided up at random between the operators, the account cards were grouped according to their place of origin. Each employee was thus given a particular geographical sector . . . ,which also meant a particular group of customers, for whom she now became personally responsible. . . . [T]he checker working opposite each card-puncher was eliminated . . . the percentage of errors had shrunk from 4

percent to less than one percent. A modification of the forms of constraint . . . increase[d] productivity. The constraint no longer appears as
the product of a hierarchical authority that imposes work rhythms from
above, but as determined by the market, and thus acquires a new sem-
blance of objectivity.

The reorganization therefore does not modify the technical content of
the work. Instead it modifies its social form. . . . The employees are no
longer confronted with the boss as the person they are responsible to but
rather with their customers and with the market.

This labor reorganization can be formally analyzed as a "democratiza-
tion" that leaves the domination of capital over labour to be exercised
through the mediation of the capitalist commodity market. This tendency
to open a firm up to the market and to consider each department as a
firm on its own subject to criteria of profitability is quite generalized
throughout contemporary capitalism (1978: 75, 76).

Thus we see how control not only operates in a process but is
internalized or becomes automatic. This is a type of control designed to manage the work process, in contrast with policy and
wage demands made by labor.

Informal control at the point of production also occurs in the
style of management that appears to offer the worker more control over the work process through "worker committees" or other
participation schemes that give workers a sense of influence over
the labor process (Henry, 1982). Richard Sennett notes how many
of these techniques are designed to elicit cooperation and "try to
create a feeling of mutual interest and good will between those
who will, in the end, give the orders and those who must obey
them" (1979: 44).

At a more general level, capital uses numerous appeals to con-
vey the idea that the objectives of capital and labor are similar—
that everyone desires increased growth, more goods and services,
and less regulation. In recent times, as the economic crisis has
deepened, capital makes stronger appeals to a unity of interest in
requesting that labor not only reduce its demands and refrain from
strikes but concede wages provided in earlier contracts in order to
protect jobs (Raskin, 1982).

In the community, an important question is how the state, as it
coordinates and plans the infrastructure of communities through

new, undemocratic administrative institutions, expects to manage
community life without jeopardizing its legitimacy. How can the
state translate power and class issues into questions about ethnic-
ity, pathology, service delivery, and interpersonal problems? People ordinarily oppose centralized, bureaucratic authority and as-
saults on community through programs like urban renewal.
Moreover, as noted earlier, the social movements that arose in the
1960s and 1970s—women's rights, anti-nuclear, civil rights, environmental—organized nationally and focused attention on the relation between local experience and broad issues such as employment, housing, health care, sexism, and racism.

In some urban areas, one response to the limits of external control has been to burrow from the inside, through an agency of the
state or an agency with some relation to the state that appears to
emerge from the community. One set of institutions that can be
defined as part of the informal state—penetrating communities and
community subcultures—are to be found in those agencies at the
local level such as little city halls, neighborhood task forces, community planning boards, and neighborhood advisory councils. John
Mollenkopf explains how "the last decade has transformed confrontation oriented advocacy organizations into neighborhood-based
social service agencies; as such, neighborhood organizations have
been integrated into the fabric of local politics" (1981: 18). These
types of organizations represented a response to the militancy of
the 1960s: challenges to economic growth; union militancy; and
organized protest around employment, housing, and race (Piven
and Cloward, 1979; Gendrot, 1982). Their objective has been,
symbolically and practically, to monitor activity in the community, provide outlets for and redirect activist energies, improve
community cohesion, and serve as a conduit to indigenous neighborhood organizations (Katznelson, 1981). They sometimes accomplish these ends by involving participants and making them
dependent on the local state. Ira Katznelson explains the Urban
Task Force in New York City in this regard:

The aim [of the Urban Task Force] was to tap street-level activists . . .
and to enmesh them in a series of relationships with the [local] administration. . . . Their principal purpose was not the solution of substantive
problems, but the maintenance of social order. . . .

At issue was the attempt to take the radical impulse away from the politics of race by the creation of mechanisms of participation at the community level that had the capability to limit conflicts to a community orientation, to separate issues from each other, and to stress a politics of distribution.

Once enmeshed in the new institutions, leaders were forced to fight for the rewards and resources these new organizations could distribute and to fight for them on the terms these organizations made possible (1981: 138, 177, 188).

These structures, as alternatives to community organizing, mobilization, political demands, community control, and other potential protest action, translate politics into a form of service delivery and the resolution of social problems (Morgan, 1981; Cockburn, 1977).

Neighborhood interests are typically expressed in programmatic terms— more funding for the service delivery organization—rather than in universal, political terms like "community control." . . . The result has been to [reduce] the basis for unity across organizations by decomposing collective issues into much more specific ones. . . . Local government incorporated and utilized the neighborhood political thrust while attempting to avoid a significant redistribution of actual power (Mollenkopf, 1981: 31, 34).

Citizens' interests are thus incorporated and institutionalized. Management criteria are applied to community issues without giving real power to the community. Community mobilization is replaced by a rhetoric from the state that emphasizes neighborhood needs, the idea of community, decentralization, and other issues in a language designed to conceal the state presence. Cockburn describes how incorporation occurs through involving citizens in forums such as neighborhood councils which permit officials to anticipate objections, reduce confrontation, and generally, "bring people into a friendlier acceptance of local authority" (1977: 109). The characteristics of these agencies I have been describing express precisely the potential effects of NDR. Much as these institutions helped to civilize and administer poverty (Katz, 1984), NDR civilizes conflict. The resolution of conflict is offered as a service, thereby disorganizing collective action.

Another example of the informal state which translates problems in the environment of capitalist social relations into individual pathology is also associated with community mental health. New forms of behavioral therapy now operate in schools, prisons, and hospitals which do not merely seek, conventionally, to help patients adjust to social life generally, but apply a specific model of capitalism that promotes the incorporation of people back into society.

Across the country experiments have been underway that entail transforming back ward life into an operational model of contemporary capitalism. In these experiments chronics who had hitherto been left largely unbothered (or simply neglected) have been placed in "token economy" programs . . . [whereby] patients earn or lose tokens (a form of money) on the basis of the behaviors they display before the institutional staff. . . . This represents a calculated attempt to replicate the prevailing economic order and to simulate its demands. . . . [T]he token economy program can be seen as an effective means of social control over potentially disruptive and noncooperative groups of troubled people. . . . Successful participation in economic affairs thus became tantamount to evidence of mental health (Neubeck, 1977: 43, 44).

Community mental health, more generally, presents itself as a helping agency offering services, usually in highly disorganized deteriorating environments. They use lay people and operate in informal settings, although funds come from the federal or state government. They redirect attention from social conditions to the effects and symptoms as experienced by citizens, redefining those conditions as stresses to be dealt with by changing individual behavior. Community leaders become involved as paraprofessionals. This may make the community dependent in that it provides a link to the state through the community. People are thereby incorporated, integrated into social systems which monitor them, coopt their power, and otherwise expropriate that power (Gamson, 1968; Brown, 1979; Donzelot, 1980).

Four contemporary concrete forms of the state apparatus can be identified to explore the penetration of social life in communities through the informal state: decriminalization, diversion of juvenile defendants, deinstitutionalization of the mentally handicapped, and public welfare. They are all more humane and less directly au thoritarian than the control systems they supplement or replace. But they also extend and intensify control in new ways that correspond to disruptions to the local infrastructure associated with changes in labor market conditions, even though they are deeply connected to the formal state.

Juvenile diversion programs, for example, represent a response to vulnerabilities associated with redundant youth who may remain dependent for long periods of time, especially in geographic areas with high unemployment, and who are likely to engage in criminal activity (Schwendiger and Schwendiger, 1976). Many of these forms, which tend to maintain, include, disperse, and essentially stabilize various social groupings rather than exclude, punish, concentrate, or ignore them, represent a form of tightly managed investment in people as human capital (Spitzer, 1979b). Their otherwise unemployed, volatile, unproductive, unconsuming position constitutes disruption to the extent that they fail to produce or consume and concentrate themselves in given settings—whether the prison, mental institution, or skid row.

A majority of states have decriminalized public drunkenness, in order to "treat" the inebriate as a health problem rather than as a criminal. Inebriates are swept off the streets (often by the police) but not arrested and therefore not protected by the principles of due process. They are taken to detoxification centers (in protective custody) and often must submit to extensive supervision by medical professionals and demonstrate their fitness to be returned to the community before they will be released.

Alternatives to conventional adjudication in the criminal justice system, such as expanded use of probation and diversion from prosecution and incarceration, allow judicial authorities to monitor offenders in a community setting. Participation in alternative programs requires cooperation with officials for periods longer than the sentences offenders would have received had they been prosecuted. Many jurisdictions use indeterminate sentences for juveniles; defendants must meet certain criteria for successful completion of the disposition. Control involves structured, detailed diagnosis, screening, supervision, reporting, and classification (Scull, 1977; Cohen, 1979, 1985; Feeley, 1980).

A crucial aspect of monitoring is that officials emphasize attitudes and habit more than facts or behavior in an attempt to prevent future deviance or conflict. "Juvenile court does not really pronounce judgment on crime; it examines individuals" (Donzelot, 1979: 110). The goal is to identify

potential pre-delinquents or high risk populations, [but] there is a deliberate attempt to evade the question of whether a rule has actually been broken. . . . [In the future] it will be impossible to determine who exactly is enmeshed in the social control system—and hence subject to its jurisdiction and surveillance. . . . The major results of the new movements towards community diversion have been to increase rather than decrease the *amount* of intervention directed at many groups of deviants in the system and, probably, to increase rather than decrease the total number who get into the system in the first place (Cohen, 1979: 346, 347).

Large segments of the mentally handicapped population are being deinstitutionalized, ostensibly in order to enhance their autonomy and enable them to lead natural lives (Scull, 1977). Many are actively supervised (if not adequately served otherwise) by professionals who monitor their adjustment to community norms rather than minister to their medical or psychological needs (Chu and Trotter, 1974). Portions of these populations are subsidized by the state to generate cheap labor for the competitive sector of the economy at a cost lower than their upkeep in an institutional setting (Scull, 1977).

Perhaps the most common form of monitoring is directed toward the poor and other surplus populations who receive monetary and service benefits from the state in return for allowing officials to scrutinize them (Donzelot, 1979). Recipients must expose the details of their daily lives for examination by social workers, psychologists, and bureaucrats. They also endure the harassment of house inspections and family interviews by public officials seeking to uncover moral or psychological defects. Many of the requirements and judgments that form the rationale for monitoring derive from concern over the alleged erosion of the work ethic and of labor markets. "Relief practices are always determined by the conditions of work among the lower classes. . . . [Relief recipients will not be treated] well as long as there are workers who are so poorly paid that they must be coerced into staying at their jobs by the spectacle of degraded paupers" (Piven and Cloward, 1971: 345–46). The welfare system, however,

is no longer just a system of social control tied to immediate labor market conditions. Rather, the displacement and integration of people in the work system . . . is increasingly controlled by the welfare system. . . . Welfare services . . . regulate the growth, structure, and development of the displaced population (Hirschhorn, 1978: 72).

Informality and decentralization extend control. Informality facilitates early intervention and prevention of social disruption. Control need not be contingent on legal violations. The "helping professional" can engage in detailed inquiry into and surveillance over private lives under the guise of assistance. Discretion is expanded. By blurring formal distinctions about what constitutes deviance, the state expands its authority to regulate (Cohen, 1985).

Community-based institutions disperse social control (Cohen, 1979; Spitzer, 1982). What this means is that deviance management and other control functions can be integrated into patterns of everyday social life, using not only social service agencies but also neighborhood groups, family members, and peers. Control operates within the plant, the office, and the community, whereas planning and decision making are centralized in the state. Problem populations need not be segregated in institutions since the whole social environment can be organized for regulation. State authority thus widens its orbit of control while disguising the explicit coercion that might generate resistance. Thus the informal state represents a shift in social management. People focus on each other not their conditions. Attitudes are more important than action. And the language is diagnostic, not political.

The informal state, similar to other forms, contains contradictions; it is a phase not a final solution. One contradiction is that incorporating citizens into a particular form of social order based on involvement and participation can lead to an expectation of greater self-government and autonomy. In Burawoy's words, "If the self-organization of workers is necessary for the survival of capitalism, it also questions the foundations of capitalism" (1979: 73). Worker participation schemes may lead to more direct challenges to capitalist prerogatives, although this issue is hotly debated (see Zwerdling, 1980; Compa, 1982). Another contradiction is that such control weakens the capacity to impose more directly hierarchical, authoritative controls in the future, which may be necessary when welfare state programs fail and further exploitation of labor is the only recourse for capital (Hirsch, 1978).

The informal state comes into direct contradiction with state planning. State planning expands instrumental technocratic reason while the informal state seeks to employ decommodified, everyday discourse and practice. To the extent that one moves outside the state to new nonstate forms of representation and intervention, the potential for resistance expands. The informal state bases its success on results not values.

All attempts to use the everyday hegemonically are ambiguous because such structures and ideological practices create the capacity for resistance and new political practice. While the state can create the forms, it can never fully control their interpretation. People may reject them or experience them in a way which leads to unpredictable outcomes. Autonomy may be desired above accommodation. And instilling the ideology of local self-management heightens the demand for its realization.

The dynamics of capitalism as a social system generate certain forms of state control in interpersonal daily life which simultaneously support and erode capitalist social relations. The mode of production and the attendant infrastructural arrangements that support it influence the specific forms that control takes. The primary propellant for change within these forms of control is class struggle. Thus, these informal processes always generate resistance and are always in flux. They remain outside of direct capitalist control and never fully resolve the problem of order. In times of severe economic decline, disorder expands and resistance to conventional control intensifies. Given these constraints, we can now begin to explore the derivation of neighborhood dispute resolution as an instance of the informal state associated with the reproduction of order in capitalist society.

PART II

NEIGHBORHOOD DISPUTE RESOLUTION AND THE STATE

CHAPTER 6

The Structure of Neighborhood Dispute Resolution

Neighborhood dispute resolution provides an opportunity to understand the restructuring of the state and the developing forms of social domination in capitalist society, as well as the potential for resistance. Part I explained how and why state power expands into civil society to regulate almost all aspects of social life. It theorized the conditions which produce NDR. The state expropriates power and authority from civil society by creating bases for legitimation with a "human face," undermining failing institutions, and concealing its authority (Wolfe, 1977). What is relatively new about this expansion is its timing, scope, methods, and immersion into what were formerly peripheral areas of interest in everyday life (Santos, 1982; Spitzer, 1979b). NDR procedures are not new but their reemergence in neighborhood forums suggests elements not present in earlier modes. These elements exemplify a distinctive form of expanded state activity. It complements and remains closely tied to the formal system. In Gramscian terms, that form of activity represents an expression of the state in civil society. A difference here is the way the state creates hegemonic structures and ideologies in its formal apparatuses. Whereas in previous historical periods the state relied on existing indigenous ideologies of the working class in a form that, in effect, said "we are the state here to help you," (e.g., social services, reform) the state now says: "we are you." NDR is offered as an agency of the community, not merely one that serves it.

I have indicated an impasse in the existing institutional and ideological capacities of the state, especially in the judicial system,

and explored developing outcomes. Given the possibilities, such
as more overt coercion, no action at all, court reform, expanding
of legal jurisdiction, watering down of rights, or creation of more
special courts, why does this particular form, with its peculiar
characteristics, emerge as one outcome of (even if not a final solution to) the impasse in forms of state political and social control?
How does NDR potentially expand state control by restructuring
and managing conflict as it does and the ways disputants' lives are
penetrated? How is informalism not only a response to disruption
but a means to create a basis for hegemony—to make citizens more
accessible to the state? NDR represents one option within a range
of options and suggests the range itself—most notably in its planned,
decentralized, informal qualities. These NDR processes represent
a decommodification of social life as it becomes overcommodified
and overrationalized by capital expansion.

Neighborhood mediation forums can best be understood in relation to the reproduction of and resistance to capitalist social order, as one way in which social relations in the community are
restructured and class relations translated organizationally into relations between individuals. As institutions of the state, they display, at the level of community, problems in reproducing the social relations of capitalism and its developing systems of
legitimation. They are not self-determinate, independent of the
social relations of capitalism. Nor are they independent of the state
and the formal legal system. NDR forums make sense only when
interpreted as political and ideological institutions of the state, even
if they are transformed or absorbed into some other system. This
does not mean that they express the direct interests of a class or
the state but that their structure, features, discourse, and practices
connect them to the ideology of a class, making their independence and impartiality impossible. They articulate class relations,
even though they are relatively autonomous from direct class control. That is, they are constituted by their own internal practices
and actions of the agencies that plan and implement them.

My objective is to explain neighborhood mediation from the
analysis of the capitalist state and hegemony in general. A central
question is how NDR forums establish hegemony in their structure and process. How do they express or fail to express the order
requirements of capital? How does less law potentially mean more

control? In order to explain what NDR means, its derivation, characterization, and possible consequences, we must return to its paradoxes, problems, anomalies, and most distinctive features.

A first paradox or oddity is that while NDR appears to be free of the traditional trappings of the state and, specifically, the judicial system, it is not. Boaventura de Sousa Santos refers to it as "a kind of state produced non-state power" (1982: 259). Its structure confuses its characterization: it *is* an agency of the state from which it remains formally segregated. It is technically nonlegal and service-oriented yet reflects qualities of bourgeois law. For example, it employs a system of rules embodied in mediator training manuals, even if they are not explicitly legal rules. Moreover, disputants engage in contract-like agreements which they sign. Similar to the traditional judicial system, mediation excludes community participation or attendance. This contradiction is related to its contradictory location in the state, combining features of the rationalized, planned state and the qualities of informalism, linked to local cultures.

A second paradox is that NDR appears as a contraction of state power—a less intrusive, passive voluntary institution—when it actually expands and intensifies state power into realms of social life not amenable to formal state control. Being voluntary and without authority it apparently possesses no power for users to challenge political injustice. However, the state expands its power over disputants by connecting itself to them through managing their actions in the NDR forum.

Another paradox is inherent in its most distinctive feature: it unites top-level centralized planning and coordination with decentralized control at its base in the community. It coopts people in their most pressing social relationships. It seeks, simultaneously, for some types of disputes, to make community or interpersonal relations of what were once legal relations and, for other types of disputes, such as domestic disputes, to make people think of their personal relations as legal or requiring state intervention.

Fourth, open-ended outcomes and voluntary participation are deemed distinguishing virtues. Yet NDR's specific methods promote a total orientation to a predefined order, although it is not immediately apparent that its processes automatically suppress working class interests.

Overall, NDR must strike a delicate balance between providing a responsive justice that does not generate a demand for democratic control, and managing a complex variety of social populations while retaining their support. A tension exists, then, between old-fashioned legitimations of Jeffersonian democracy and the requirements of the modern corporate state. This characteristic makes it vulnerable to challenge and to disintegration or transformation.

Given these paradoxes and others, NDR's characteristics make sense not as an institution designed to achieve justice or even to resolve disputes per se, but as an organization of crisis management that arises from the same problems that generate changes in the state that have already been described. NDR is not a system of collective justice or popular justice. It does not respond to citizens' conflicts as they are experienced. On the contrary, NDR generally fails to help people as members of a social class; rather it manages, shapes, and directs social conflict in a particular way such that the collective and political basis of conflict is defused. It institutionalizes conflict within a particular conception of social order. As such, NDR is an alternative to politics as much as it is an alternative to courts and the rule of law. However, NDR remains a paradoxical institution precisely because, as in all other institutions of capitalist domination, it possesses elements of liberation from capitalist control. These liberatory elements, referred to in appeals to potential disputants, are defining features of its ideology. Some qualities of NDR mobilize people by bringing them together face-to-face in a negotiating position, encouraging cooperation. Other elements individuate and disorganize them. Unraveling its hegemonic qualities is made difficult because NDR is not the product of direct class confrontation but only prompted by class contradictions.

Thus we must distinguish between appearance and reality: between how the neighborhood program and its agenda is presented to the community and disputants, and its meaning as an institution of the state within capitalist society. How does it construct and impose a view of social reality? While this question cannot be answered conclusively, we can demonstrate how the ideologies and practices of the neighborhood dispute resolution center enter into the lives of individuals and communities, given the boundary conditions and structural constraints inherent in the institution, and the ways in which values and practices of the disputants influence the process.

The central conclusions concern (1) the way in which informal justice in a neighborhood setting can serve the general interests of capital, without necessarily solving its problems, through a local, seemingly respresentative process; (2) how power is exercised and experienced in a variety of ways through a process and not necessarily through content or outcomes; (3) the way informal dispute resolution, which means less reliance on the rule of law and more reliance on ad hoc direct state action, permits the management of populations formerly constrained by the rule of law and that such necessary management is facilitated by neighborhood mediation; (4) how the discourse of conflict in mediation and its structured processes inform us about the nature of social order; (5) the way in which informal dispute resolution is a means of penetrating and disorganizing the community in which it operates—how the state uses community culture against itself, similar to other organizational forms that disorganize the working class; and (6) the contradictions suggesting that NDR is unstable and must fail as it is constituted, creating opportunities for an oppositional conception of justice.

I also consider how neighborhood dispute resolution forums establish hegemony—both from the top down in the structure and from the bottom up in their processes, how they represent an expression of class struggle, and why, given their contradictions, they are not a solution to the problems of order and class conflict.

Before presenting my interpretation of NDR, I need to describe briefly the central structural features of mediation important to the analysis and characterize (as an ideal type) a typical mediation process. In all cases, mediation will refer to informal dispute resolution programs as organized by the state or institutions connected with the state, primarily in the judicial system, in contrast to community-based justice (see Wahrhaftig, 1982; Shonholtz, 1984). The following descriptions suggest only the most general, visible components common to most mediation.

THE CENTRAL FEATURES OF MEDIATION

Although mediation programs vary widely on almost every feature, including objectives—some aim to reduce court caseloads;

others emphasize access to the judicial system, problem solving, and reduction or prevention of conflict—they share basic features important to the analysis (see Marks et al., 1984; DeJong et al., 1983; Tomasic, 1982; McGillis and Mullen, 1977; Sander, 1976).

Types of Cases

Most cases involve disputes between individuals, in contrast with those where organizations may be a party. Thus, neighbors, family members, landlords and tenants, and consumers and sellers constitute the disputants. The majority of programs stress the importance of handling disputes where there is an ongoing relationship between the parties. Depending on the program, the cases may be characterized as criminal, quasi-criminal, or civil (usually misdemeanors or small claims), although some programs specify or predominate with one type or the other. They can include such categories as problems with neighbors, money, minor property damage, domestic quarrels, harassment, trespass, consumer matters, assault, and landlord-tenant problems, among others.

Approach to Resolving Disputes

The most prominent approach to resolving disputes is mediation, which is opposed to arbitration or conciliation, a method requiring an independent third party (mediator) who facilitates or guides the interaction between disputants in order for them to reach a mutually acceptable settlement. The mediator seeks to generate discussion between the parties, interpret statements, and suggest options.

The most important feature that distinguishes neighborhood mediation from both ordinary adversarial procedures and labor negotiations is that the parties themselves engage in mediation, not their representatives. It is a "face-to-face" process.

Mediators

Mediators are typically lay people who receive special training in mediation techniques. These people may be law students or professionals in related fields such as psychology, behavioral science, social work, or law. Some programs employ full-time professional mediators. Some are paid small stipends, others perform the service on a purely voluntary basis. A great number of mediators are trained by professional organizations such as the American Arbitration Association and the Institute for Mediation and Conflict Resolution, although many programs create their own training apparatus.

Sponsors

Sponsors may be agencies within the judicial system, such as a criminal justice planning agency, court, or prosecutor; agencies of local government which might include the mayor's office or the department of human relations; or private organizations with connections to the official court system, such as bar associations or the American Arbitration Association. I refer to all these types as state-organized or official programs and they are the focus of this analysis.

Agreements

Agreements are ordinarily put in written form with specific details, signed by the parties, and witnessed by the mediator. They may require restitution, or promises to end harassment or contact, to refrain from making noise, or other behavioral options. The mediator actually writes the agreement document, checking with the parties about its language and reading it to them. Agreements may involve restitution or a promise to change or desist from certain behavior. They are usually nonbinding but a breach may lead to the initiation or continuation of a court action.

Hearing Procedures

Hearings are typically conducted in an informal setting for no more than two or three hours at most, depending on the problem. Usually they occur within a week of the time a complaint is filed. No fixed rules of evidence apply. Witnesses and attorneys are discouraged, although not always formally excluded. The objective of the hearing is to facilitate communication between the parties. Hearings have no binding effect.

The Mediation Process

The process begins with a referral from another agency which first learns of the conflict or a direct request for service by one or both of the parties. Next, an intake officer interviews each of the parties about the problem. If one party initiates a complaint, the program staff seek contact with the other party, requesting her/his participation, usually by mail. In the mediation session, the mediator begins with an explanation of the process, the mediator's role, and expectations from the parties. Then, each party has an opportunity to report her/his version of events, without interruption. Mediators discuss the issues with the parties, try to determine the problem and elicit what each party wants as a remedy in order to reach a settlement. Sometimes the mediator might caucus separately with each party. If agreement occurs, each party signs the agreement.

PLANNING AND STATE POWER

One of the extraordinary features of many neighborhood dispute resolution programs is the way in which the centralized, nationally based institutions, planned by the state, appear to emerge from the community as decentralized entities. They offer a collective, social form of legitimation for a noncollective, nonparticipatory process and reinforce the pardox of a planned activity administered on an ad hoc basis. In this sense, they share features of other community-like institutions of the informal state described earlier and demonstrate historical ties to more generalized planning within the judicial system and the state. But what does it mean to say that neighborhood dispute resolution forums are planned?

Planning is the "rationalized" aspect of mediation, and represents the most visible form of the state—through coordination and in the rhetorical appeals designed to gain support for NDR and instigate people to use it. The most distinctive aspect of NDR planning is the centralization of authority and the decentralization of function. Centralization here refers to national models, the systematization of informalism, and the control asserted by professional organizations and state planners. The centralization of authority and decentralization of function parallels the logic of corporate planning and state planning more generally.

Nancy DiTomaso, in a study of the U.S. Department of Labor, explains how the combination of decentralization of function and centralized authority obscures the basis of power.

Precisely because hierarchy concentrates power, it also makes it more "visible." In hierarchical organizational structures, the locus of power is more easily identified than in dispersed organizational structures. When the locus of power is more visible, then the "point of change" is also more easily identified. Therefore, under conditions of resistance from subordinate classes, a diffusion of power or decentralization may be the "best" means to maintain the existing relationships of domination—all other things being equal—because decentralization scatters the point of change (1978: 84).

This type of analysis may be applied to neighborhood mediation. The activities of such dispersed organizational structures have much less visibility than courts. Their locus of power is not as easily identified, even though most state-funded dispute resolution programs either are directly regulated by judicial authorities or are dependent on them for cases. The state thus retains its monopoly over justice and expands its capacity to regulate diverse populations.

More important, the decentralization of function, apart from obscuring the basis of power, also potentially secures control more effectively in practice, by expanding technical capacities and reducing political resistance, if it succeeds. For example, it is not absolutely necessary to house people in large institutions in order to watch them closely (Jankovic, 1977; Cohen, 1985). Modern technology available to an NDR program and to social service professionals (computers, information systems, surveillance equipment) permits monitoring by community-based facilities. The state is relieved of the burden of a recalcitrant, intransigent group of patients or inmates who might organize and demand legal rights.

The range of control of the dispute resolution centers, like that of other modern mediating institutions, might be limited by the effects of the growing fiscal crisis of the state. In James O'Connor's view, for example, the state can experience difficulty in its capacity to manage the social crisis caused by uneven development and increasing social demands (O'Connor, 1973). But these forums do not require large expenditures or extensive planning (NIDR, 1986). They may be established fairly quickly and inexpensively because their implementation does not always depend on a legislative act or a judicial rule, actions which are needed to restructure the courts or create new social programs. The flexibility achieved through decentralization of function and the expansion of discretion in the NDR program thus permits the state to penetrate certain private aspects of civil society that become problematic for reproducing the social order.

Over time, the extension of centralized state power, no matter what its institutional form, is likely to reveal itself as an apparatus of the state. This is so because of the inherent tension between the requirement of managerial efficiency within the state and the pretension to community-owned justice—similar to the problems identified by Wolf Heydebrand (1979) in the judicial system, more generally, between the system's administrative requirements and the judge's role as a provider of justice. Richard L. Abel expresses the dilemma for informal mediation more directly.

[C]entral control undermines the autonomy of local institutions. . . . [T]he state, in the name of informality, destroys indigenous, traditional informal justice and substitutes institutions that serve to extend central control, implement national programs, enhance the legitimacy of the official legal system by appearing to improve access, and undermine local community (1982a, vol. 2:5).

The Planners

The planning of NDR typically occurs within the state apparatus. The impetus for and design of these forums, as well as determinations of who can make what claims, begin with government administrators and judicial authorities, acting in cooperation with large foundations, criminal justice planning agencies, and professional organizations such as the American Bar Association,

American Arbitration Association, the National Institute for Dispute Resolution (NIDR), the Society for Professionals in Dispute Resolution, and associations of state and local governments (Wahrhaftig, 1982; Garofalo and Connelly, 1980a; Tomasic, 1982; NIDR, 1984). Some projects are sponsored publicly by agencies of the court system or local government. Examples include the Columbus Night Prosecutor; Community Dispute Resolution Centers of New York; The Court Mediation Service, Portland, Maine; The Neighborhood Justice Center of Atlanta, Inc.; and the Miami Citizen Dispute Settlement Center. Half of all programs are funded by local governments or the justice system and about 30 percent by private sources (Delappa, 1983). Policy decisions in many of these programs are made through the sponsoring agency, usually with an advisory board consisting mostly of public officials, bankers, business representatives, foundation vice-presidents, and representatives of community organizations. Many projects have no advisory boards; there is rarely even the pretense of community influence, particularly after they become institutionalized. This is true of projects in Miami, Chicago, and Columbus, Ohio. Some programs (Denver Center for Dispute Resolution; Community Dispute Program of Delaware County; Brooklyn Mediation Project; Citizen Dispute Settlement, Toledo; Family Dispute Services, Minneapolis) were sponsored privately through foundations, organizations such as the Institute for Mediation and Conflict Resolution, or local bar associations. Privately sponsored projects have advisory boards with community representation, but they often lack formal policy making authority. Many develop close links with judicial agencies in order to receive a sufficient supply of cases. Planners are aware that, without strong connections with agencies that can provide referrals, few cases will enter the program (Merry and Silbey, 1984). But more importantly, without such ties, programs would lack control over the cases themselves (Klein et al., 1978; Harrington, 1985). These programs sometimes appear to be connected to community organizations, but control remains in the hands of professionals with strong ties to the judicial system and other agents of the state (Wahrhaftig, 1982). Community members are represented on the boards of directors of many dispute resolution centers, but overall authority for planning and policy remains in the hands of traditionally powerful organizations and public officials. The Atlanta Neighborhood Justice Center, for example, "operated under the guidance of a Board of Directors composed of court officials, attorneys, and a few representatives from the police and community agencies" (Cook et al., 1980: 12). Moreover, the developers of these forums and court officials maintain close supervision over them; they do not relinquish control to community organizations, although such organizations could begin to challenge the management of NDR.

Neighborhood dispute resolution forums do not develop from community-based movements or from the deliberations and demands of indigenous populations. As in other government agencies and planning bodies, local participation in creating the dispute resolution programs is an institutionalized process. The role of the public generally and users specifically is mechanical, formal, and perfunctory—not democratic (Wahrhaftig, 1982). Support is normally sought only among key public officials (Tomasic, 1982). And as Bryant Garth suggests, describing the Law Enforcement Assistance Administration's (LEAA) original Neighborhood Justice Centers, "substantial participation by disadvantaged groups may be even less likely once the justice centers pass the experimental stage and are subjected to political pressures by local powers" (1982: 197). The absence of user participation may limit support in the future if the institution falters from lack of funding. Describing the early LEAA-sponsored programs, Benedict S. Alper and Lawrence T. Nichols report that, for each, the board (of directors)

seeks endorsement for the aims of the center[s] from local merchants and landlords and from other business and community groups, as well as from local government officials, including the judiciary. It strives to reach agreement with local merchants and landlords for securing their participation in mediation for specific types of complaints, such as shoplifting and landlord-tenant disputes (1981: 209).

If neighborhood dispute resolution forums were truly popular and responsive to community needs, there ought to be some evidence of popular demand or some data on community conflict that would justify their formation and structure. A community rationale does not exist—population characteristics do not require it and no key indicators, for example, disintegration of the community or user demand, demonstrate a need (Harrington, 1980; Tomasic, 1982). No significant research was conducted as a prelude to the proliferation of these institutions. Citizens may demand better quality justice, effective enforcement of rights, and speedy justice. But they do not necessarily demand the highly rationalized, state-sponsored models of informal dispute resolution, organized by experts, as *the* vehicle to accomplish their goals.

Once mediation programs begin, they usually must engage in extensive public relations activities to attract a sizable caseload, unless they resort to court referrals (Harrington, 1984; *Dispute Resolution*, no. 6, 1980). According to a report published by the Department of Justice and the National Institute for Dispute Resolution:

If alternative methods of dispute resolution are to gain widespread acceptance, incentives will have to be found both to establish appropriate programs and to use them. . . . [I]t is likely that there will be resistance to these new vehicles. Incentives will have to be developed for lawyers and clients alike to ensure the acceptance and use of alternatives to litigation. In addition, the programs' financing will remain precarious unless largely publicly supported. (Ad Hoc Panel, 1984: 19, 20)

Some research suggests that people would rather go to court than mediate or choose to resolve their dispute in some other way (Merry, 1979; Davis et al., 1980; Harrington, 1980, 1984; Buckle and Buckle, 1982; Merry and Silbey, 1984). These institutions can be established through social formations outside the state. Disputants could (and sometimes do) organize mediation projects or other methods to solve disputes themselves; it is not a scientific or complex process (Community Board Program, 1981; Shonholtz, 1979; Wahrhaftig, 1982; NIDR, 1986: 5).

Instead we find bureaucratic planners, sometimes drawn from the federal government, local bar associations, or foundations, imposing principles of conflict management and mediator training, and providing detailed blueprints for dispute resolution systems. No evidence exists that these centers represent rational solutions to people's real problems or a rational solution to social order.

Popular justice and collective justice operate from very different premises (Cain, 1984; Buckle and Buckle, 1982; Issacman and Issacman, 1982; Reifner, 1982; Brady, 1981; Santos, 1977).

Target Populations and Purposes

The poor, unemployed, women, and ethnic minorities constitute a large proportion of disputants in many programs (Goldberg et al., 1985; Cincinnati Institute of Justice, 1984; North Carolina Bar Association, 1985; Harrington, 1985; Neighborhood Justice Center of Atlanta, 1986; Cook et al., 1980; Snyder, 1978). Fred Delappa (1983) indicates that on a national basis almost 80 percent of dispute resolution programs are in cities with populations over 100,000. Fifty percent are in cities over 500,000. Ironically, although advocates claim that NDR provides a source of access to justice for those ordinarily excluded (Alper and Nichols, 1981), these populations can more accurately be considered targets of planned interventions (Snyder, 1978). They represent a major element capable of generating disorder and mobilizing for social change and are located in highly volatile and impoverished neighborhoods.

Community residents may participate in state-sponsored dispute resolution forums, but they are not designed with their interests in mind (Kidder, 1980). Rather, the objectives belong to corporate planners, professionals, and public officials, "concerned to ease community and interpersonal tensions" (Alper and Nichols, 1981: 134) and otherwise prevent people from overburdening the courts. As one program director in Florida commented, "We're a safety net for the criminal justice system" (Interview, 1979). The language of a Ford Foundation report reveals these concerns:

Our capacity as a people to resolve conflicts is under severe strain. . . . There is strong evidence that the number and complexity of disputes will continue to increase. . . . What is needed is a systematic approach that expands our understanding of the larger issues in conflict resolution . . . and helps to de-escalate conflicts. . . . The changing nature of legal rights and entitlements might also be examined—how these changes affect the adversary system (1978a: 64).

Reducing social conflict was an objective in the early LEAA Neighborhood Justice Centers, as well as other programs that followed (Cook et al., 1980; Singer, 1979; Snyder, 1978). A Ford Foundation newsletter reveals some of its interests in establishing mediation experiments: "A major aim of the experiments was to reduce the heavy burden being placed on the courts and regulatory bodies by environmentalists, consumers, tenants, prison inmates, and other groups that were increasingly using the legal process to defend their interests" (1983: 2). In Cleveland, a project was established in an area "once known for its cohesiveness but now experiencing increasing fragmentation and disorderliness (*Dispute Resolution*, no. 7, 1981). A draft planning document for the National Institute for Dispute Resolution also expresses the political anxieties directly.

The period since World War II has seen an enormous growth in the number and intensity of disputes in the United States. The growth of population, its concentration in cities, and the complexity of society give rise to conflict and divisiveness. Many institutions that have traditionally mediated conflict have become weak and ineffective. . . . Courts are overloaded and administrative agencies overwhelmed.

Divisiveness has visibly marked the past two decades. . . . In the United States we have witnessed riots by minority populations, tensions between different groups, and a steady rise in the demands of a wide variety of organized interests—women, environmentalists, consumers, farmers, prison inmates, and many others—for equal rights, redress of grievances, and a larger voice in national decision-making (NIDR, 1981: 1).

The uniform nature of many forums and the desire to institutionalize them suggests, too, that the goals of program planners are cosmopolitan not local. The U.S. Department of Justice specifically sought to establish a program plan that could be replicated anywhere (Alper and Nichols, 1981). The objective of the federal government has been "to formulate a coherent national policy on the resolution of minor disputes" (Alper and Nichols, 1981: 207). And the National Institute for Dispute Resolution contends that

a national focus is needed for experimentation, evaluation, coordination, and dissemination. [Many of the activities in dispute resolution] are being conducted largely in isolation. They lack the conceptual and operational focus essential for maximum effectiveness and systematic reform (NIDR, 1981: 6).

Such planned coordination denies the historical, local qualities that differentiate communities. It also demonstrates the emphasis on the homogenization of conflict that characterizes NDR planning.

Public officials concerned with maintaining order, avoiding time-consuming public debate, and assuring the uninterrupted management of growth have suggested that neighborhood dispute resolution forums may have something to offer as a response to social order disruptions. "One selling point is that a properly developed center could be a buffer for elected officials in such diverse areas as housing, welfare, code and zoning violations, and animal control" (*Dispute Resolution*, no. 4, 1979: 2). The performance goals of the Mountain View Rental Housing Mediation Program in San Francisco included reducing pressure "on small claims courts, police, and other complaint agency intakes" (*Dispute Resolution*, no. 4, 1979: 8). Another project emphasized the savings to taxpayers and noted that mediation would "consume less wage-earner time" (Pinellas County Citizen Dispute Settlement Project, 1978). The objectives set by planners are also evident in the criteria used for evaluations—the number of cases entering the system, the capacity to keep cases out of court, disputant satisfaction, and the number of cases resolved (Roehl and Cook, 1982). The major stated rationales are presented in the language of cost-benefit analysis: savings for courts, less time wasted for professionals, and smaller caseloads. Anthropologist Sally Merry, for example, comments on the evaluation of the three Neighborhood Justice Centers sponsored by the U.S. Department of Justice:

There is no clear evidence in the whole NJC study about the impact on the community. The goal of community development was not seen as a priority. . . . They could have considered a greater sense of control and sense of resources available to community residents . . . or collective action on community-wide problems and people beginning to perceive their problems as community-wide and not individual . . . or translation of individual grievances to social action (1982a: 56).

Many of those who testified in the congressional hearings on minor dispute resolution in 1978 and 1979 can rarely be identified with the needs of disputants—for example, the United States Chamber of Commerce, the National Association of Counties, the National Center for State Courts, the Motor Vehicle Manufacturers Association, the National Housing Federation, Sears Roebuck and Company, and the Better Business Bureau (U.S. House, 1978; 1979). As Robert L. Kidder notes, programs planned outside communities "express the interests and generalized perspectives of various parties seeking to influence centralized governmental policy. These parties include economic institutions, politicians, government bureaucrats, and professionals acting as advisers" (1981: 428). These influences that Kidder describes explain how, for example, informalism can be understood as a response to the growth of consumer and tenant rights, rather than an attempt to meet social needs (Lazerson, 1982).

Planners of dispute resolution, then, are not community residents and users of the forums. They are usually not tied to the community in any way, nor do they involve themselves with other basic concerns of the community. Producing social justice is not a goal. Planners generally stress the prevention of conflict, reducing delay and the overload on the judicial system, reducing claims against the state, the difficulties of making rational judgments, the complexity of disputes, and the need for consensus. Their actions and agendas are not ones which suggest attention to disputants' needs, but rather a concern to eliminate or minimize certain conflicts or challenges as inappropriate, dangerous, or threatening to an undefined conception of social order.

Coordination

As stated in an early planning document for the National Institute for Dispute Resolution:

The Institute will have made a difference if it helps convert what is presently a fragmented *ad hoc* series of initiatives into a coherent, unified approach—an approach that will build a structured capacity for negotiation and consent into American society (NIDR, 1981: 13).

Planners focus on managing the tensions in communities that may lead to either the destabilization of social life or organized protest that can expand the boundaries of political action. All of these concerns indicate striking parallels with corporate planning more generally—especially the emphasis on system overload and the need for coordination.

Similar to urban planning, the organization of dispute resolution from centralized agencies is a means for handling the disruptions within the local political system and urban environments which partially result from economic dislocation and the advancement of substantive legal rights. NDR thus responds to the threat to order and the types of disruption that cannot be divorced from protecting the urban infrastructure for capital.

Coordinated planning within court-based programs represents an expansion of the state through a centralized apparatus with extensive, previously untapped resources.

Because of attachment to the court, the program has access to the state computer, technical assistance, on-site visits, and . . . books. Uniform standards and guidelines can be set for training curriculum and operating procedures. The [New York] programs also have recognition as a program that contracts with the chief administrative judge and this increases acceptance by the justice system and the average citizen (NIDR, 1984: 5).

Many NDR programs coordinate what were once formerly discrete sources of control directed at different social populations. That is, what are usually treated as separate problems by separate agencies, for example, health, education, family problems, can now be interrelated in common tasks in maintaining social order (Morgan, 1981; Donzelot, 1979). These agencies, through the judicial apparatus, are now brought to bear under a central auspice to regulate conflict in a more systematic fashion. For example, many dispute resolution centers now rely heavily on social service agencies and police for referrals and as places to refer disputants (Ray et al., 1986; Ray and Clarke, 1985; DeJong et al., 1983). The resolution sought by a mediator may require one or both disputants to contact a network of social service agencies that diagnose and monitor them over an extended time (Ray et al., 1986; Delappa,

1983). A mediator in Florida explained the process in her program this way: "If I think there is an emergency I will refer someone right away. If they need personal counseling, I wait to see the outcome of the hearing. Usually I contact the referral [protective services, family counseling] agency and make the contact for the party (we have a list of agencies). The party must call but I give the agency the name to let them know they're coming" (Interview, 1979). These referrals are typically understood by some mediators as cures for or assistance with other problems that relate to the dispute. In some forums that accept quasi-criminal or even noncriminal disputes, the parties sign a legally binding document in which they agree to work with social service professionals in employment, counseling, and educational settings.

Possibly the best example of active coordination through centralized services, linking mediation with other formal state apparatuses, is found in a model referred to as the Multi-Door Courthouse. As proposed by Professor Frank Sander of Harvard Law School, and practiced through experiments in some large cities, the multi-door approach offers many types of dispute resolution services in one location which diagnoses disputants' problems and refers them to the appropriate site for further action. In this highly institutionalized arrangement, police, prosecutors, and other social service agencies refer people to the Multi-Door center which tailors people's problems with precise, specialized solutions (for a detailed account, see Ray and Clarke, 1985).

With the creation of more informal, community-based systems of control, such as the neighborhood dispute resolution center, people who were once ignored by institutions of control because they violated no law or could not be effectively regulated are potentially engaged by them (Cohen, 1985). Their problems are socially disruptive for capital as we have indicated, but not in a way that previously could be readily managed. Informal dispute resolution processes develop a connection between individuals and an official state process that otherwise would not have existed. A description of the Urban Court Program in Massachusetts notes that

in cases where outside assistance can benefit the parties, the terms [of the agreement] may call for participation in alcohol, drug, marital or individual counselling. Clients are also directed to housing placement, employment training, health or other human service agencies (Crime and Justice Foundation, 1979: 3).

An evaluation of the Brooklyn Dispute Mediation Center also argues for coordinated interventions.

Mediation might be more effective if it were made the first step in a sustained series of interventions. Such a program might involve repeated mediation sessions, counselling, and other social services if mediation is to realize its potential as an effective alternative to the prosecution process in cases that most need an alternative (Davis et al., 1980: 65).

What planning accomplishes overall, to move beyond the impasse in control, is the rationalization, institutionalization, and homogenization of conflict. What were once historically separate areas of control now come together through the state, employing fairly uniform models of dispute resolution. These models are geared toward treating all conflict in the same way, regardless of content. They generalize what is particular. The rationale, at one level, is order maintenance (Harrington, 1980, 1985). The method is to create hegemony through selfcontrol, by using symbols and discourses embedded in everyday activity. Planning deals with one element of social order described in chapter 1: to sustain working-class populations and inhibit destabilizing reactions to dislocations resulting from market forces and other planned restructuring of the social environment by capital.

Contradictions

As in other realms of planning, planning NDR creates contradictions. The first such contradiction concerns the politicization of justice. To the extent that the scope, procedures, and personnel of community justice can be the object of struggle, then people might reappropriate justice from state planners and professional organizations. For example, the NDR concept may suggest to citizens that institutions other than courts, with less authority, can handle some of their problems. Since NDR lacks a history and ritualized norms embedded in the formal legal culture, the organization of

NDR would appear more open and flexible as organized by ordinary citizens.

Second, because NDR forums are novel institutions, the process of planning them may offer a public forum for questioning the foundations of the legal system and debating the interests behind and consequences of selecting a particular procedure or policy. In practical terms, NDR's vulnerability occurs in the balance that must be struck between providing a forum that does not lead users to demand more from this institution on their own terms while offering a particular sense of order about handling conflict in communities by involving the participants in the procedures. But even apart from collective demands, NDR is open to ideological challenge because it does not rely solely on symbols but on an open-ended process open to public debate. Moreover, the newness of the institution, its flexible procedures, and citizens' perceptions that derive mostly from the traditional judicial system generate expectations that cannot always be met. According to a mediator in Miami, "they [disputants] feel they're going to get justice. They don't understand mediation" (Interview, 1979). It is therefore highly vulnerable to transformation from below that may lead to expansion of extralegal methods of protest and community organization around collective interests.

At the same time, community residents can learn skills in negotiation, mediation, and advocacy that enhance their legal and political competence. NDR forums embody, in principle, the characteristics that would define them as community-oriented, for example, community solidarity, responsiveness, and self-management of disputes. This potential for popular justice is a contradiction, an aspect of its dialectical quality. NDR handles conflicts that disrupt labor power: sustaining its circulation and reproduction without tensions that interfere with it in everyday life. Similar to other aspects of the informal state described earlier, it involves people in a process disassociated from their governing that process while simultaneously suggesting, in the process itself, that citizens control it. There is also a contradiction between the rationalized character of planning informal dispute resolution and the appeals required which vitiate its objectives. Its romanticization of community is a basis for its undoing. Thus the potential for undermining NDR as planned by the state is inherent in its central features.

CHAPTER 7

The Informal State and Neighborhood Justice

The direct imposition of social control through state planning and traditional state apparatuses represents one basic element of control. Imposed control in NDR entails coordination and rationality that defines the structure of the mediation process from sources external to the parties. At this level, it is organized to manage social environments (see Spitzer, 1982; Hirschhorn, 1978). Its orientation is directed toward the modification of behavior and the internalization of values to suit immediate social conditions, rather than values themselves. The law restricts judicial options in processing cases and makes it difficult to tailor responses to community circumstances. Informality allows dispositions to be adapted to a specific social purpose. I have indicated the ways in which the structure of mediation is generally, if indirectly, linked to the social reproduction requirements of state and capital, but in a contradictory fashion which creates the possibility for a liberatory potential.

Informal dispute resolution is also a way of incorporating citizens into the social order through a decentralized state institution, embedded in the ordinary processes of social life. Part I referred to the way in which the state colonizes peripheral areas of social life with greater intensity through the informal state. Informal dispute resolution is another mechanism by which the state enters the community to deal with disorder and to create a basis for hegemony. It sometimes accomplishes this in the way its practices become equated with the general interests of society and the particular needs of communities. As a disguised, quasi-bureaucratic police force that places itself between social classes it may stabilize as well as invade community life. Such a mechanism resolves risking the use of infiltrators and becomes, like federally-funded community action programs in the 1960s, a means of developing an indigenous monitoring agency. But unlike some new forms of incorporation which integrate citizens into conventional politics, the neighborhood dispute resolution forum potentially creates an alternative to any kind of political action. And, also unlike some other state-sponsored community institutions, these forums employ a new type of procedure in an arena normally understood as externally imposed—the law. Thus, although decentralized state forms are not new, they are relatively new as applied to informal justice because the rule of law as exercised within the judicial system is traditionally a visibly imposed form of control.

NDR is not merely linked with the informal state; it is itself an agency of control. Moreover, informal dispute resolution represents a reassertion of more traditional forms of community-based social control but without any organic connection to the social environment. NDR asserts the neighborhood as the source of justice within a procedure that falsely signifies the community as the basis of authority. It offers a rhetoric of community, voluntarism, and participation that is highly institutionalized without appearing to be. This is precisely what Gramsci argued was a necessary condition for hegemony: to represent the popular demands and aspirations of subordinate classes as part of the project of capital. Without a utopian element (e.g., community, self-help, cooperation) it could not succeed (Santos, 1982). A forum is created that offers an alternative to the neighborhood, community organization, union meetings, or other social movement activity in which collective action might occur. It also represents a means to create hegemony: to gain the active consent of subordinate classes to the social order. Specifically, it incorporates people to an understanding of what constitutes conflict and how it must be handled. Thus NDR is an institution oriented toward consent and not merely managing disruption.

The informal state through neighborhood justice is explored at two levels, first as it operates as a force on the community as a whole, as directed by state planners. Second, it is explored as practiced on individual disputants within the mediation process—

the informal features planned at the top but legitimated at the bottom which incorporate disputants into the social order without the overlay of direct coercion, threats, formal rules, or propaganda.

To understand the ideological framework for mediation, I will briefly mention its basic assumptions about conflict. These assumptions are embedded in the discourse and practices of mediation (Folberg and Taylor, 1984; DeJong et al., 1983; Ad Hoc Panel, 1984). They also appear directly in programmatic materials and literature designed to enhance the use of mediation. The assumptions regarding conflict are:

- conflict is generally not good and there can be too much conflict in society; settlement is good;
- conflict is individual and personal rather than contractual or political;
- conflict is primarily a problem in communication or a misunderstanding rather than an issue of interest or power; and
- most conflict, whatever the content, ought to be treated by the same methods, based on general psychological principles.

The assumptions regarding mediation are:

- mediation is a community institution: it comes from and belongs to citizens;
- mediation can also create, empower, or restore community;
- mediation offers choice: it is a voluntary process, a free exchange;
- mediation is the best (and sometimes the only) way to resolve conflict; and
- mediation is efficient and effective.

The application of these assumptions will become apparent as the appeals and inducements for mediation are examined. They represent both aspects of stated and unstated rationales for mediation, as well as concepts that implicitly guide the process itself.

HEGEMONY AND COMMUNITY

Control through the community at first appears to be an oddity because the community, traditionally a force against capitalism, now is used as a form of self-control. Citizens enter neighborhood mediation at the level of the state's logic not their own participation or authority. The neighborhood mediation program is made to appear as a representation of the collective, of the community, rather than as an obvious form of alien authority which citizens normally resist and recognize as administrative control. It is managed by agents of the state but administered by lay people trained in its techniques.

NDR is presented to the community as if it is *of* the community. We need to explore how this occurs in the planning of mediation and the way it is offered to the public—prior to the process. For mediation to work people must suddenly become aware that they have conflicts, that an agency exists for solving them, and that the agency is really themselves working with a mediator. A central question is how the state invades the community, uninvited, and how, in Abel's words, it "renders the disadvantaged more accessible to the state" (1982a: 258). This can prove especially difficult, given that these dispute resolution institutions are not organically connected to neighborhoods, and derive from interests and agendas not especially related to the body politic as a whole. On the other hand, it may be enticing to people who ordinarily fear involvement with the judicial system, as a result of high costs, time, and a lack of knowledge. A staff member in the Ft. Lauderdale program noted that mediation "is fast, free, personal, and without guilt or penalties" (Interview, 1979). This is a major characteristic of its seductiveness.

Three elements or ideological appeals for informal justice that occur prior to the mediation process are identified: the rhetoric of involvement, popular justice or the helping agent, and community empowerment. Each of these contains both ideological and practical elements which cannot be separated. The purpose in all cases is to capture people's attention, and to draw them into the institution of their own volition in a manner distinct from formal, legal, bureaucratic agencies.

Involvement or participation, a first element, refers to those actions or appeals that seek to include people—providing them with a sense of access, opportunity, and efficacy. Sometimes the planners of dispute resolution programs openly express the way in which community participation is necessary as a means, not only of securing community support, but to enhance the likelihood that potential disputants will use the program and achieve resolutions. As James H. Klein and others have argued, "The broad involvement of community agencies is vital. . . . Since the participation of both disputants is voluntary as is compliance with the resolution reached, community pressure is one means for achieving both of these goals. Thus, community support for the Center must be obtained" (1978: 42–43). In specific appeals to potential parties, strong emphasis is given to the sense of opportunity available to solve a problem through disputant-controlled decision making. Appeals to participate are found in newspaper accounts, planning documents, and program brochures such as the following from Houston, Texas:

Maybe you are having a dispute that you can't seem to work out. Perhaps it is relatively minor, or perhaps you are considering going to court or calling the police to file a complaint. Or, perhaps a complaint has been filed against you. You can now choose to settle the matter quickly and without cost through the Neighborhood Justice Center. The Center offers parties in a dispute a chance to explain their side to an impartial mediator. Mediators are trained to help people reach a lasting settlement. They do not force a solution. Instead they help people reach their own agreement. If the parties cannot agree they may still pursue the matter in court. A mediation session is scheduled only if all parties voluntarily agree to participate (Neighborhood Justice Center, Houston, Texas, 1980).

This is an example of the appeal to access as opportunity, a chance to do it yourself. It implies the inappropriateness and ineffectiveness of initiating action within the formal system, by portraying it as alienating and time-consuming.

Emphasizing the use of lay persons as mediators is another method of involving citizens, which suggests that the programs are seeking to represent the community. For example, a staff member in St. Petersburg stated that "disputants have a sense that they can play the game too—not by lawyers' rules" (Interview, 1980). However, the planners' rationale for using lay mediators, even though they are sometimes costly to recruit and train, is to educate and win the commitment of disputants to mediation (Klein et al., 1978).

A second aspect of hegemonic ideology at this level is the presentation of the NDR as a form of popular justice and a helping institution—to be differentiated from legal, professional, or bureaucratic institutions—and one that offers justice more simply and inexpensively, with less stress. Indeed, descriptive program materials often note the superiority of mediation by appealing to people's fears about the criminal justice process, emphasizing the irrationality, failure, and likely dissatisfaction that can occur in the courts.

Most people really do not want to take friends, relatives, or neighbors to court. They rarely wish to . . . have someone pay a fine or perhaps even go to jail (Wilmington Delaware Citizen Dispute Settlement Center, 1979).

The money and emotional costs of litigation often exceed the benefits to be obtained. . . . Often litigants must spend more money to seek "justice" than is at issue. . . . Great time delays . . . leave many disputants with unresolved anger (Center for Dispute Resolution, Denver, 1980).

Instead, programs emphasize how mediation solves problems with a helpful mediator who will not take sides.

Instead of staying angry, involving the police, feeling helpless, or going to court you can call the Albany Dispute Mediation Project. It's useful. . . . It's free. . . . It's convenient. . . . It's confidential (Albany Dispute Mediation Program, 1980).

In a third aspect, the idea of community empowerment first occurs in the title of many programs, for example, the "neighborhood" or "community" justice center. Appeals to community empowerment in state-sponsored programs are usually implicitly suggested by reminding disputants that mediators have no sanctioning power and that the parties decide the results. Although many of the appeals emphasize self-reliant communities, community empowerment, the general affirmation of the neighborhood as the basis for justice, and an alternative to impersonal forms of law and government, no evidence exists that any government-sponsored program has been established to accomplish these ends or achieved them (Garofalo and Connelly, 1980b: 606; Shonholtz, 1984).

What all of the orientations share is the notion that conflicts involve problems in human relations not law (Greason, 1980), and certainly not class. To the extent that citizens use NDR, they are potentially diverted from expressing discontent through other political and community organizations—whether complaining to a local consumer protection agency or engaging in a rent strike. And, as Roman Tomasic argues, "the neighborhood justice movement clearly can be seen as serving a legitimizing function and consequently deflecting or diverting criticism of the formal legal system with its significant inequalities" (1982: 246).

THE INFORMAL STATE, HEGEMONY, AND THE DISPUTANT: THE MEDIATION PROCESS

Hegemony in a process such as mediation is very different from that secured by technocratic-administrative control which people increasingly reject (Katznelson, 1981). It differs too from direct cooptation because, rather than integrating citizens into a conventional political process, it eliminates politics altogether. Disputants may internalize the values embedded in the process. And what they internalize is a conception of conflict, social order, and community self-help that potentially disorganizes and limits the possibility for collective action by manipulating and diverting attention. The process in mediation is different than popular justice—what people do for themselves without the state (Santos, 1982; Buckle and Buckle, 1982; Spence, 1982), or a more explicitly defined collective justice (Cain, 1984).

The informal state, in its present form, applied to sociolegal relations is a relatively recent phenomenon and transcends anything that the judicial system and legal rationality were ever established to handle. Regardless of its legitimating functions, the formal judicial system is primarily a form of externally imposed control when applied to interpersonal conflicts. The basic element in the transformation to informalism concerns the shift noted earlier from actions imposed by an outside agent, such as a judge, to domination through a face-to-face process. Instead of people confronting the law as legal subjects within an external agency, which creates problems of legitimation, they confront *each other* through an institution in (but not of) the community, analogous to social service agencies. But NDR is more than this. It is self-regulation: the community controlling itself.

Informalism creates a localized form of power inherent in the process of mediation and not merely the outcome (Mather and Yngvesson, 1981). The law is not an instrument of control; rather, legal relations themselves constitute the hegemonic system. Hegemony is embedded in the mediation process as the division of labor constitutes, in its elaborated form, domination over the labor process and therefore domination over the labor class, independent of state and other forms of private power. Through informal mediation, the state burrows from the inside within an agency free of traditional trappings of the state. For example, similar to the way in which a company union controls workers (Henry, 1983) or the way in which a prison warden uses inmate culture as a device for inmate control, informal community dispute resolution represents the state controlling the disputant, but without the conventional trappings of the state.

Instead, as I shall indicate, neighborhood mediation programs use a system of collective social legitimation for what is in reality a hegemonic process primarily designed and implemented by public officials. This is its essence. The mediation process disguises its administrative, order-maintenance rationality and disguises the social process of everyday life by the way it presents conflict—as interpersonal and particularistic. The politics of the informal state can be understood in its class context by exploring the mediation process and its components, and how that process meets or fails to meet its own imperatives or boundary conditions in order to create hegemony. The central questions are: What makes informal dispute resolution a form of control? How do its practices potentially create hegemony? What are its contradictions? An understanding of the workings of NDR must begin with the idea that it constitutes relationships, rather than merely managing them. It organizes patterns of interaction and thereby creates meaning through its patterned elements.

There are at least four characteristic elements or components that define the process, similar to those described in chapter 5: (1) the appearance of disputant control through involvement and participation of the parties; (2) the definition of conflict as interpersonal; (3) the resolution of disputes by consensus and accommodation; and (4) the appearances of everyday life in discourse and interaction through an administrative procedure. For each of these components it is necessary to demonstrate that they are elements of mediation, what makes them potentially hegemonic, how hegemony is established, and the implications. Equally important, I want to demonstrate how each moment of hegemony provides a liberatory moment—the potential for progressive transformation through resistance, based on the contradictory, paradoxical nature of mediation. The case material derives from program documents, mediator training manuals, and transcripts from mediation sessions.

Within the discussion of each element is also an analysis of how legitimation is constructed for mediation through the mediation process. Once the legitimation or acceptance of the process occurs, it can become hegemonic. For our purposes, legitimation is constructed when the disputing parties (a) interact in the process and its outcomes without question—that is, the parties agree tacitly (by participating) not to challenge the process regarding how disputes will be resolved, and (b) resolve a dispute through a binding resolution that ends the dispute: both parties accept the result. Hegemony, then, involves a collaboration with the process, using the symbols and language of everyday life.

Mediation must accomplish these two objectives in order to be successful and retain its identity. Within the structural conditions, there is great variability. However, the interactions during a mediation session can only be understood in so far as they confirm the structural boundary conditions of the process and do not violate them—for example by interrogating disputants or imposing a solution. It is necessary to negotiate not only the result of a dispute but also the terms of its resolution. The legitimacy of a dispute develops through a rule arrived at in the process and by which the parties can conduct themselves. That rule is not a legal rule. It develops *in the situation* in response to the features of the situation that could not be predicted in advance since no one knows what the parties will be like or exactly how they will interact. (See Sudnow, 1965, for an analysis of how organizational perspectives in the criminal justice process, rather than predetermined logic, influence the rules of the system.) These features, when we find them, guarantee that NDR meets and confirms its boundary con-

ditions—those conditions that define the phenomenon as mediation and not a formal legal procedure. If over time, for example,
mediation programs began to define rights or rules of evidence,
they would violate the characteristics that define the process as
mediation. To the extent that this occurs, mediation undermines
its own ideology. The patterns of interaction, without recourse to
external forces or other structures, now guarantee the legitimacy
of the process. This is part of what it means to say that legitimacy
is internal to the process. Legitimation cannot be assumed in advance from the official rules for mediation or anything we know
about capitalism, hegemony, social control, or prevailing legitimation mechanisms. Informal neighborhood mediation, as part of
its definition, requires relatively autonomous institutional forms
which cannot be predicted in advance. If the source of domination
is recognized, it limits the potential for hegemony. Mediation is
not necessarily a rational response to the specific conflicts that come
to the attention of NDR centers, although the nature of the exchange within them is in part organizationally required by the rules
of mediation, implicit and explicit.

The Illusion of Disputant Control: Managing Disputes through Involvement and Participation

Advocates of mediation contend that mediation is a disputant-
controlled process, in contrast with the courts, whereby the parties actively devise agreements on their own terms (Folberg and
Taylor, 1984; North Carolina Bar Association, 1985; McEwen and
Maiman, 1981; Sander, 1976). This construction is inaccurate (Felstiner and Williams, 1978). Mediation is a highly structured, nondemocratic (if informal) process, dominated by its prespecified rules
and the capacities of mediators to manage disputes. The rule of
law is replaced with another set of rules, less explicit, which embody a definition of social order. As Richard L. Abel notes, in
these informal institutions

conflict is confined by clearly demarcated, relatively rigid boundaries. These
are temporal (conflict has a definite beginning and end), spatial (conflict
may only be waged within certain arenas), . . . institutional (jurisdic-
tional rules ensure that only one institution will have competence), stra-

tegic (violence is prohibited, rhetoric may be restricted), even linguistic (certain forms must be used) (1981: 253–54).

Moreover, the precise way in which disputants are engaged in the activity is an aspect of its hegemonic power. On its surface, if mediation is to be accepted as a legitimate process, disputants must believe they influence it, that it belongs to them. They must trust the experience. Hegemony depends on a process that provides a strong sense of participation and involvement, whereby disputants are heavily invested in its success. That involvement, typified by the practice of face-to-face bargaining in order to reach "mutually acceptable agreements" constitutes an important aspect of hegemony. Why? Because, as we shall indicate, disputant control and a "free exchange" between the parties is an illusion. The perpetuation of that illusion sometimes enables the state to manage conflict and secure control without conventional resistance. The belief that one has achieved a solution by consent, without external authority, provides a sense of responsibility and therefore legitimation in the experience. The pressure to settle is not interpreted as pressure or persuasion. Participation can generate consent to the rules of mediation similar to the way in which some applications of participation operate in the labor process (Burawoy, 1979) and in community service agencies (Katznelson, 1981). Disputants are constituted as subjects of mediation within clearly demarcated meanings of participation, much as they are constituted as legal subjects in the courtroom.

I want to demonstrate, first, that disputants do not control mediation—that it is not, in its practice, a free, voluntary exchange. Second, I want to consider how its dynamics as a process falsely present the appearance of disputant control when involvement is passive, not affirmative.

In order to demonstrate the first point, it is necessary to show that there are structured rules that guide mediation (and the intake process) and that the mediator is not a passive referee but an active participant, instructed to keep matters focused and to define boundaries for interaction (Davis et al., 1980). In Leonard Riskin's view, "The mediator is managing the communications process . . . [and] must intervene carefully at the correct moments" (1982: 36). According to a study by the Vera Institute of Justice, the mediator was "an active participant . . . reinterpreting disputants' perceptions, steering the parties towards what the mediators believe to be fair and effective solutions, reinforcing social norms of how relationships ought to be conducted and providing emotional support to those who needed it" (Davis et al., 1980: 44). Each instance of mediator discretion provides an opportunity for conflict and resistance by the parties. Mediator decisions are therefore political decisions, which can be indicated by examining guidelines and practices.

In the supposedly disputant-controlled mediation session, a common partial set of instructions to mediators about how the process operates suggests how mediation is highly structured and managed. It is excerpted from a manual for mediators in landlord-tenant cases.

MEDIATION MODEL

SET GROUND RULES
A. Time limits.
B. Rules of common courtesy.
C. Interaction rules: i.e., please direct your conversation to me rather than to each other.

PARTIES PERCEPTION OF THE PROBLEM
A. Let each disputant tell his/her side of the story. . . .
B. Re-state the problem in simple, concise language and be sure that each disputant agrees with your perception of the problem. . . .

DEFINE THE BARGAINING RANGE
A. Ask the disputants the following two questions *before* beginning any negotiation efforts:
    1. What are your goals for this mediation . . . how would you like to see this matter resolved?
    2. What/how much would you be willing to give to see this matter settled this afternoon?

NEGOTIATION
A. If the parties bargaining ranges do not meet, begin working on issues—generally going for the easiest ones most likely to succeed.

RESOLUTION
A. State the settlement verbally, ask if that is what they both agree to.

B. Write up the settlement in very specific terms, include dates, amounts, method of delivery and penalties, if appropriate. Have each disputant read the contract before signing it. . . .

THE ROLE OF THE MEDIATOR

1. Provide structure to the conflict
2. Control form of conflict
3. Active listening
4. Help them communicate
5. Balance the power
6. Control the tension level and readiness to bargain
7. Reward for good faith concessions
8. Impartial but empathetic
9. Keep ultimate responsibility for solution in their hands (Martinson, 1981: 13, 15).

Each of these instructions represents a restriction and a boundary on the process, allowing mediators to position disputants and organize the session. They may prove effective for reaching a settlement, in the terms of mediation, but not necessarily for meeting the disputants' needs as individuals or members of a larger social class. The simple rules of common courtesy could obstruct a full airing. In addition, disputant goals may evolve in the process; an initial statement may not be clear. More important, the instructions invalidate the idea that mediation empowers people. The contract, in this context, is an assertion of the mediator's (state's) symbolic authority and threat of sanction. The nine listed instructions defining the mediator's role establish the mediator as the key player, directing every move, playing upon the participant's anxieties about the conflict. Another statement of guidelines excerpted from a program in Ft. Lauderdale, Florida, indicates the character of psychological management more fully.

GUIDELINES FOR CONDUCTING A SUCCESSFUL HEARING

1. Make an initial statement that each party will have an opportunity to be fully heard without interruption. This will ease some of the tension and should help the respondent feel less defensive.

2. Attempt to secure an agreement from each party that they will remain silent while the other person is telling their side of the story.
3. Assess the emotional state of each party.
4. You are a catalyst to get the parties to arrive at a mutually agreeable resolution. Minimize guilt or innocence and maximize communication.
5. Try and keep disputants calm. If one or both is getting extremely upset, try and calm them down by asking that they lower their voice, or sit back in their chair or slow down their rate of speech. Identify the action that they are manifesting that indicated they are upset. Do not just say, "Calm down."
6. Some rules for listening that may be helpful include:
   A. Attention responses such as "Uh huh," "OK," "I understand." Do not approve or disapprove, but acknowledge person's remarks.
   B. Echo responses where you may repeat key words or phrases. This will facilitate word flow in the proper direction and limit rambling.
7. Ask questions, however, use open ended questions rather than questions that can be answered "yes" or "no". Do not ask questions that are too broad. Try and focus questions on the main problem.
8. After everyone has a basic understanding of the problems, it is time for the mediation state of the hearing.
   A. Try to encourage and guide parties toward suggesting their own solution.
   B. Do not prescribe a solution or try to impose your values on them.
   C. If all else fails, make a specific suggestion that does not favor either party if possible.
   (Citizen Dispute Settlement Program, 1979)

Notice, in the Ft. Lauderdale guidelines, the number of references to managing the emotional state of the parties: "attempt to reach an agreement . . . that they will remain silent"; "minimize guilt or innocence"; "try to keep disputants calm"; and so forth. These are not instructions which immediately appear necessary or relevant to handling conflict. Maybe the parties need to express emotions that the mediator guidelines attempt to suppress.

These guidelines are also indicative of the extraordinary attention to the details of language and behavior that establish mediator trust and control. They apply a variety of psychoanalytic strategies that deny disputant control, in assuming that the parties can be appropriately sidetracked, overemotional, or negative. In fact, what a mediator might interpret as respondent defensiveness may be a sign of appropriate resistance to the process. Each guideline allow mediators to narrow the range of possible discourses and outcomes, obscuring and delegitimating alternative agendas. At the same time, such an organized plan, embedded in the ground rules, the signing of the agreement, and other rituals, helps to establish the overall legitimacy of mediation.

The guidelines represent another example of the way in which NDR replaces punishment with supervision, blurs the distinction between the public and the private realms of social life, and otherwise expands state power. Implicit in these guidelines is a belief in the incompetence of people to resolve their own conflicts, unimpeded. Mediators are not necessarily aware of these issues in the course of their work.

There are many guideline manuals in other programs that elaborate similar approaches to mediation (Crime and Justice Foundation, 1980). What appears as a spontaneous process is thus a precisely rationalized procedure, with many details structured in advance and a response prepared for almost every contingency.

The directive role of the mediator in channeling the dispute, as well as organizing its character, is illustrated by this description of a program in Miami, Florida:

At the mediation session the complainant airs his view of the dispute first, followed by the respondent. The mediator listens without trying to narrow the issues right away but rather listens for what appears to be the underlying roots of the conflict. . . . The mediator gives assurance to both sides, encouraging them both to open up. The emphasis is not on therapeutic counseling but rather on getting the parties to talk through their dispute, and to grasp the reality of the other side's position. . . . The mediator encourges the disputants to identify possible solutions to their problem (Klein et al., 1978: 86).

A mediator in Miami indicated some of the subtleties of directing the process in response to a question about the inequality of bargaining power that sometimes arises.

I will oversee the interests of the weaker party. If someone is taking advantage, I will bring this out to the weaker party. . . . The idea is to balance the relationship and not just be neutral (Interview, February 1979).

The mediator's manual prepared by the Crime and Justice Foundation in Boston demonstrates, in its introduction describing the material covered, the extent of mediator control:

The trainers will present the various techniques used by mediators to determine facts, remain objective, establish trust, . . . search for the best offer, narrow issues, funnel discussion, encourage the disputing parties, act as an agent of reality, create the desire to settle, suggest hypothetical terms, maintain order, and word a mediation agreement.

Strategies should be developed for the rest of the hearing—such as pursuing information gaps, preparing questions for each party, establishing a sequence for private meetings with each party and rehearsing the things to say when a disputant enters the room again (1980: 2, 13).

In a section on settlement techniques, the manual asserts: "mediators will sometimes wrongly allow themselves to be steered away from key issues by the disputants" (1980: 43). It does not make sense to say that mediators can be wrongly steered away from key issues if the process is disputant-controlled. An examination of Houston's Neighborhood Justice Center clearly states that mediators "facilitate communication while maintaining control of the hearing. The mediator implements a negotiation strategy" (Neighborhood Justice Center of Houston, 1986: 7). William L. F. Felstiner and Lynne A. Williams contend that many mediation sessions' outcomes are not "formulated by the disputants, as the ideology alleges, but [occur] because a mediator was alert to a feasible adjustment in a destructive cycle of interaction" (1982: 228).

In their study of the Urban Court program in Dorchester, Massachusetts they also found that

the training is ambivalent about manipulation and coercion. On the one hand the trainers stress that free choice is a value—agreements last because they originate with the disputants. Yet, the trainers also indicate that disputants are to be maneuvered into an agreement by the use of ambiguities, by suppressing conflict in later stages of a session, and by the coercion of the alternative to an agreement, whatever that might be (1982: 117).

The mediator training material in Ft. Lauderdale's Citizen Dispute Settlement Program included the following description which in-

dicates control, however benign its intention, and how the mediator will deflect resistance before it arises.

It is to the advantage of mediators also to understand the psychological
process. CDS provides an opportunity for both parties in a conflict to be
heard in the presence of an "authority figure" (the mediator). This ability
to explain their side of the story fulfills their psychological needs to have
their view "acknowledged". . . . Once both parties feel satisfied that
they have been able to voice their view, then about 90% will be willing
to mediate. . . . It is important that *all* communication go through the
mediator. This insures that the level of emotions is under the control of
the mediator (1979).

The opportunity for mediator management is enhanced because
most parties do not have experience or understand the culture of
mediation as they do legal culture. Concepts about judges, due
process, rules of evidence, and winning and losing are embedded
in the culture. They do not have to be explained. The newness of
current NDR centers limits the capacity of parties to know they
are being managed, how they might challenge the process, or how
they might organize it differently. Resistance to mediation emerges,
in part, because it is unfamiliar and challenges ordinary assumptions about conflict resolution. A mediator in St. Petersburg, Florida commented,

I let them agree to things easily at first and then probe. I set the tone for
what's to follow and show them how to do it, how to agree, step-by-
step (Interview, 1979).

Another in Ft. Lauderdale remarked,

If we aren't getting anywhere I'm going to direct them, to get a solution
to it. I'll say: "Won't this be good?" (Interview, 1979).

A mediator in Miami noted,

Sometimes, the parties get confused. They say: "Why don't you decide?"
They say: "Why can't you make them [the other party] do this?" Some
think I'm a judge, even though I tell them I'm not (Interview, 1979).

ᴄertain elements of mediation give the appearance of disputant control—that disputants create the norms and guide the process in a free exchange. To understand these elements we need to consider how disputants are involved and control is established in such a way that they willingly participate while simultaneously disarmed, their power diminished. Control is constituted in the roles, rules, rhetoric, and individuation of the process.

The blurring of role distinctions is a primary element. Mediators present themselves as passive, neutral parties without much authority, when in fact most mediators are trained professionals coordinating the entire procedure, concealing their exercise of authority. Some sense of how mediators establish their role that conveys an impression of equality with the parties—the friendliness, informality, and neutrality—may be gleaned from the introductions given to disputants in the following excerpts from case transcripts.

My name is E. S. I am a mediator. I have no authority to make a decision. I'm not a lawyer or a judge. I'll make suggestions about what I think is fair. (Transcript no. 1, Portland, Maine, 1980).

My name is E. S. I am a mediator. I'm not a lawyer or a judge. I'm here to bring you two together and talk and see if we can solve this. . . . So that we will know what it's all about, will you be willing to tell us what your claim is? (Transcript no. 2, Portland, Maine, 1980).

What we do here is we bring together people who have a problem and we talk about it. I act as a facilitator. I bring the parties together and to an agreement that is acceptable to both parties. I'm not a judge, I don't try people. I'm not here to find out if anybody is innocent or guilty. All I'm here to do is resolve a problem. OK. The rule that we follow is that the party that brings the claim speaks first and the other just listens. And then the other party has a full opportunity to respond. (Transcript no. 3, Portland, Maine, 1980).

The mediators, in stating their name and role are beginning to establish informality in a way that involves the disputants. In stating "I'm here to bring you two together," the level of the dispute is immediately shifted from an adversary procedure to a joint, participatory action. This is important in establishing legitimacy:

that the case will be solved and that settlement is *the* objective. The disputants, later on, are introduced personally, not by their roles or legal definitions such as claimant or defendant.

Mediators establish themselves not as state representatives but as helping agents. As part of the introduction to the process, the mediator or intake officer prepares the parties with statements that soften their resistance to participation. This aspect is fairly routine. One intake officer in Florida commented:

I tell them [the parties] it's voluntary, not legally binding, that there is no judge, that it's informal, that no one will be found guilty, that we cannot impose solutions but only suggest options. But they must understand that *they* must explore the problem. (Interview, 1980).

Prior to the mediation session, mediators and other program officials sometimes explain to the parties that their reason for being there is by choice: to preserve the relationship between the parties, to avoid court, and to behave rationally. Thus, the staging rules, symbols, and context disarm disputants and trivialize the authority of the mediator in their eyes. The institution is simultaneously made powerless for the disputant—no due process, no rights, no audience—while the state is made powerful in dealing with the disputant by making the exercise of power invisible. The mediator's guidelines are not routinely indicated or made available to the parties.

In the process, disputants are made to feel that they have a stake in it, that it belongs to them, and that it is fair. For example, the mediator at one point in a typical case says: "OK. What's your side." The parties accept this practice of full airing; first one side then the other. The mediator has further established informality and begins to establish fairness. The parties do not question the process, either by leaving or seeking to specify their own ground rules. In another exchange, one of the parties says: "I'd like to make one more point." The mediator replies: "Sure." He does not say: I'll allow that, nor does he interrupt. This also conceals control and helps to establish hegemony. Mediators are instructed never to interrogate or appear to interrogate the parties. For example, in a mediation session in Los Angeles in January 1980, two roommates are disputing. One (F) charges that the other (P) locked her out of the apartment. The mediator then says to P: "Do you want to respond to F's charge?" The mediator does not say: "Did you do this?" which would suggest interrogation. The Crime and Justice Foundation mediator manual warns mediators specifically: "Phrasing questions in an accusatory manner may be very destructive to the mediation process. Questions of this type include—"Didn't you do that? Who did that? Why did you say that? What were you doing that night?" (1980: 33).

Mediators make an effort to support each speaker through interpretation and verification stating what has already been said to establish fairness, but more importantly to give focus and direction to the situation. For example the mediator states in one case: "I guess what this whole thing revolves around is . . . ," or: "So you (P) were really violating company policy. . . . " All of these procedural gestures are not necessarily in the interests of the parties because they are a portrayal, a false construction of reality. The Crime and Justice Foundation mediator manual explicitly demonstrates this point.

Reassurance is a technique, which if exercised skillfully, contributes significantly toward the momentum to settle. The mediator should compliment each disputant's sincerity, reasonableness, and patience. . . . Every disputant should be stroked. . . . Timing and subtlety are very important (1980: 41).

Such manipulation challenges the idea of a free exchange controlled by disputants.

Even apart from direct or indirect manipulation, it is the structural context that distinguishes mediation from a free exchange. It has nothing to do with the good intentions of the mediator. For example, a conversation between a student and a college professor about a thesis, however mutually beneficial and rewarding or friendly in its appearance, is influenced by the power one has over the other to validate the final document and by the system of university rules about what constitutes an acceptable thesis. Similarly, a mediator finally decides when a case is settled, organizes the conversation, and remains bounded by training in the rules of mediation.

Thus, mediation functions within a context of cultural values and a system of rules which establishes an irrational power relationship. The rules are hegemonic because they restrict and direct the organization of the experience in the situation, while giving the appearance of something else. Mediation is not therefore truly a free, voluntary, self-managed, informal interaction, although it appears to be so. A contract process is in effect. This contractual relationship is established at the outset: a bargaining among equals or volunteers, unlike legal processes. There is thus an objective and subjective dimension of the tie of neighborhood dispute resolution to the state and the state to the disputant through the mediator. The objective dimension is that the state can coordinate control at the top through planning, in order to control detailed aspects of life, by bringing a certain form of scrutiny to everyday life. The subjective aspect of hegemony is, from the standpoint of the parties, that individuals begin the process as equals and as volunteers in relation to each other and the process. And the dispute resolution center affirms in its practice that contract is the fundamental relationship, but not in the sense of commerce. It is the idea of contract or relationship that Karl Marx [1867] (1967) noted is affirmed in the workplace when a so-called free laborer negotiates a free contract with the capitalist. It has the look of a contract when it is not. Why not? The individuals involved are being regulated by rules designed within the state apparatus, even though it appears as a free exchange. Ironically, although mediation is presented to the public as an alternative to the abstract "legal subject" which is itself a fetish or commodification of social relationships, so too is mediation. It simply takes another form. And these contextual features of informalism cannot be suspended, even if the mediator tries to do so. They are intrinsic to the process (see Sudnow, 1965). The management of disputes means specifying what details will be considered, predetermining what can be bargained for, making every activity accountable, although it appears reflexive. The authority of the mediator as manager is absolute. And the absence of reflexivity makes it absolute.

An important aspect of social domination in mediation concerns the way in which disputants are invested in and fulfilled by the experience. It is part of the meaning of involvement in the process. For example, many of the postmediation program evaluation questionnaires ask: Did disputants feel they had an opportunity to participate? Did they have an opportunity to tell their story? Was the mediator fair? Did the mediator pay attention? (Roehl and Cook, 1982.) High ratings on this question are found in many programs. In the Brooklyn Dispute Resolution Center 77 percent of defendants and 73 percent of complainants were satisfied (Davis et al., 1980). In the Neighborhood Justice Center of Los Angeles 94 percent of those interviewed expressed satisfaction with the Center's services (Neighborhood Justice Center of Los Angeles, 1985). Almost 85 percent of the participants in the Cleveland Prosecutor's Mediation Program reported satisfaction with the program and believed it was fair to their side (Cincinnati Institute of Justice, 1984). The Denver Custody Mediation Project reported that 93 percent of clients would mediate again (Pearson and Thoennes, 1982). Project evaluators are also careful to ask disputants about the personal qualities of the mediator (Roehl and Cook, 1982; Davis et al., 1980). The majority of disputants typically say they found the mediator helpful. The Janice Roehl and Royer F. Cook study of the LEAA Neighborhood Justice Centers found 88 percent to be satisfied with the mediator, as well as the overall experience. James Garofalo and Kevin Connelly (1980b: 591), examining the results of numerous programs across the country, conclude "that dispute resolution centers are creating favorable impressions among the parties who go through the mediation process." But one must be careful about interpreting surveys on disputant satisfaction (Harrington, 1985: 142–43). Asking disputants questions about their feelings toward mediators may be interpreted as a process of legitimation. Client satisfaction is vital not merely in a general way to achieve legitimation, but as a means to ensure continued use of the institution and continued willingness to follow up on the agreement and referrals.

Craig McEwen and Richard J. Maiman, in a positive assessment of the participatory aspects of mediation, note that "the sense of obligation derives in part from the power of internal controls, people's desire to act consistently and to live up to commitments that they themselves had made voluntarily and more or less publicly. 'I said I would pay; therefore I will pay.' The power of these internal controls as a source of compliance has significant implications for social policy as well as for sociological theory" (1981: 267). McEwen and Maiman assume the reality of participation and that reducing "resentful obedience" through coercion is good for the system's legitimacy. It is precisely the internalization of order in a process of false participation that creates hegemony. Because the disputants (in the process) and the community (in the structure) do not shape the discourse, interaction, and moral direction of mediation, it becomes an alien institution which expropriates power from people. The rule of law is also alienating but without the suggestion that its rules come from a participatory process. NDR does not merely rhetorically or symbolically claim disputant control. It creates a practice in a form which provides an experience of control in the "doing" of mediation.

Defining Conflict as Interpersonal

A fundamental characteristic of bourgeois law, embedded in legal principle, is its emphasis on possessive individualism, on individual responsibility. Ordinarily, the principle of individual responsibility is undermined in the movement toward bureaucratic authority, service delivery, and therapeutic treatment. That is, state intervention, in dealing with various social populations en masse and approaching so-called social problems on a broad scale, obliterates individual distinctions or reliance on formal principle (Unger, 1975). For example, unemployment is understood and sometimes treated as a structural problem of the economy, beyond the capacities of any given unemployed person to affect.

However, in state-sponsored neighborhood mediation, similar to the formal system, the social basis of conflict is ignored, even though responsibility and blame are explicitly excluded as the rationale for outcomes or decisions. Although one individual disputant is not culpable or guilty, each disputant *is* the problem—the cause of a disruption to the social order not the conditions under which they live. Ironically, whereas traditional notions of popular justice normally incorporate the community context and social conditions in seeking a just outcome (Santos, 1982; Spence, 1982), mediation normally excludes such considerations (see Reifner, 1982). Disputants can technically raise any question or issue. But the content of conflict is divorced from collective interests, segregated from similar cases, and limited to the immediate relations between the disputants. For example, a dispute between a landlord who owns a large apartment complex and a tenant is treated as a conflict between two individuals, but not as rights-bearing subjects with a contractual relation. In this sense, it differs from the formal system. Hypothetically, such a conflict might be dealt with by discovering how many other tenants experienced similar problems with the landlord, what the effect of such disputes was in the neighborhood, and whether either side violated rights of the other. Without such connections, potential collective issues are decomposed. Neighbors who might advocate for change and discover common concerns never interact with one another.

Whatever the issue, the disputants are directed down a path which emphasizes the unique, interpersonal conditions of their case (Harrington, 1985). Solutions involve compensation, redress, and behavior change. Mediators rarely attempt to connect cases to recurrent experiences that others have had as members of a social class, precedents for decision making, or to aggregate events. If they did, it would violate the boundary conditions defining mediation and create potential legitimation problems. And as Abel remarks, "most significant interaction in contemporary society occurs outside the residential neighborhood. The latter rarely contains the antagonistic dyads of capitalist and worker, producer and consumer, polluter and pollutee. . . . Just as the forces of oppression . . . extend across neighborhood boundaries, so must the organizations of resistance that are fighting for distributive justice and social change" (Abel, 1982b: 289). One cannot challenge prices, profit margins, investment decisions, or the content of the food supply in NDR. People do not experience these things directly. But NDR inhibits a vision of the totality by translating and defining conflict at the level of the individual. The social relation between the parties and the transformation that must occur for a successful outcome is the transformation of the disputants rather than any social conditions or institutions in which they live. Their motivations and perceptions are the basis of analysis.

This individualization of conflict, isolating the subject, is an aspect of hegemony precisely in the way it conceals the social context, narrows the framework of conflict, and limits options for interpretation by the parties. Legal principle is translated into psychological and personal terms, focusing on behavior rather than entitlement. Conflict becomes private, excluded from public scrutiny and made irrelevent to a public interest or, more directly, to a class interest. The mobilization of public law is inhibited. But nothing inherent in informalism necessitates an individualistic perspective.

Defining conflicts as interpersonal is facilitated by the way in which mediators encourage dependency on the mediation process, even when mediation is not necessarily in the parties' interests, or when they reject mediation. Mediators rarely support responses other than settlement. They typically will not advise the parties about the advantages of a lawsuit or filing a complaint with an agency of government. For example, the mediation manual for the Commission on Community Relations Landlord-Tenant Mediation Project provides these instructions:

Don't Get Involved with the Law: Talking about the law can be counterproductive. If one of the disputants insists on bringing up the law, just say, "We are not here to try to 2nd guess the court. We are here to come up with a settlement that you both can find satisfactory (Martinson, 1981: 14).

This is an instance of moving disputants away from concepts connected with rights, justice, and contract and toward identifying themselves as the source of problems. As in the case of the workplace, the organization of the mediation process itself structures conflict; the parties take responsibility for conflict—it is theirs alone. They are educated and disciplined to a way of thinking about their condition and each other that excludes any institutional or wider focus. The mediator often asks each party: "How would *you* like this case to be resolved?" rather than discuss legal or political remedies applicable to the situation. Program evaluations stress benefits for individuals rather than impact on communities (Garofalo and Connelly, 1980b; Merry, 1982a).

What are the implications of redefining conflict as interpersonal? There are certain similarities between the individualized, fragmented character of handling neighborhood disputes through an informal process and the nature of control in the work process. Harry Braverman (1974) describes the rationalization of work and its reduction to abstract labor. The division of labor is comparable to the dissection of social conflict into interpersonal disputes, torn from the holistic nature of social life and divorced from the discontent generated by poverty or work conditions. Consider consumer disputes. Consumers may "win" cases as individuals by getting their money back or obtaining the repair of a product, but they lose as members of a wider social class interested in preventing a recurrence of the incident or effecting a change of policy. NDR thereby dilutes political power.

For example, a dispute about the safety of a product purchased in a supermarket would be transformed into an issue between a dissatisfied customer and a local merchant rather than be interpreted as a more fundamental conflict of interest between producers and consumers, with implications that may affect the whole community. This restructuring of conflict parallels administrative solutions to conflict in the workplace, where the refusal of a corporation to install necessary safety equipment is translated from a question of safety or owner responsibility into an issue of compliance with work rules, a dispute between a worker and a plant manager, or a claim for compensation (Edwards, 1979). Personalization of conflict can fragment common concerns and the capacities for collective action. Udo Reifner, describing the transformation of legal advice in prefascist Germany, remarks how "atomized and integrated into a strange procedure, clients became the objects of a process aimed not at advancing their interests but at avoiding conflicts" (1982: 110). We could speculate then that some complaints might lead to coordinated activity for social change or other political action that would change conditions. Hassles with noise, for example, might lead to demands that landlords or city planners use insulation or revise building codes. Overall, then, interpreting conflicts as disputes between individuals "implies that a particular remedy for each case is all that is required" (Cain and Kulcsar, 1982: 393). It limits the connection between personal troubles and public issues, thereby transferring the social crisis into individual failing. In this sense, NDR promotes the decline of community.

Consensus and Accommodation: Narrowing the Locus of Conflict

The method of resolving disputes in mediation is through accommodation in order to achieve consensus between the parties rather than by a judgment of right or wrong in an adversarial setting, with winners and losers. The objective is to tame or civilize conflict. Parties settle their controversies but do not justify their actions according to legal, ethical, or moral norms. In mediation, there are no norms at all, only behavioral styles and linguistic codes, emptied of political content. Deliberation becomes unnecessary, a hindrance to settlement. Mediation, interpreting most conflicts that it handles as misunderstandings, emphasizes compromise, peace, the futility of struggle, order, and the illogic of confrontation (Abel, 1982a; Snyder, 1978; Cook et al., 1980). As one mediator in St. Petersburg, Florida indicated, "mediation is a process for reasonable people. . . . When they start moralizing it's hard to get an agreement" (Interview, 1979). A major objective is mutually satisfying, lasting outcomes and the prevention of future conflict. This contrasts with advocacy and representation which are traditional objectives sought by those demanding access to the courts and the satisfactory resolution of claims.

How is seeking consensus a form of securing and obscuring control? How does a consensus model change the meaning of a conflict? Consensus operates as hegemony by directing disputants toward solutions and away from rights, issues, values, collective problems, or what might be in the best interests of the parties (Fiss, 1984). NDR transforms conflicts into problems of communication through its own professionalized jargon. To the extent that it secures consent as a taken-for-granted objective or as a necessity identified by disputants—rather than an imposed subordination—it has achieved hegemony. Indeed, McEwen and Maiman (1984), in their study of mediation in a small claims court, found that "consensual processes lead to social psychological pressures for compliance that are not associated with authoritative judgments." Consensus is constructed by the mediator through the discourse of mediation. To the extent that the parties are involved and do not question the rules of mediation, consent is achieved. Consent fails when the parties refuse mediation or withdraw.

The following excerpt comes from a mediation session in Portland, Maine in 1980. It concerns a problem about the repair of a truck. The parties failed to reach agreement. However, this excerpt suggests the way in which the mediator directs the parties away from the issue of right and wrong and toward a consensus, even though the owner of the truck (P) clearly contends that the evidence or facts support his position. The mediator does not consider the interests of the parties as they see it, but instead stresses that mediation is the only sensible way to handle the situation.

Mediator: You are saying that it [the problem] wasn't caused by tightening the manifold bolts improperly?

R: We could argue that for a long time.

Mediator: So this has cost you [P] $642. to get your truck working again, right?

P: Yes.

Mediator: There's no way I can say what's right here; I don't know. I don't know if anyone on this earth knows.

P: I'd like to point out a fact that hasn't been discussed yet. I have here a sworn statement by the mechanic who repaired the truck that the problem was caused by the manifold bolts not being properly torqued.

Mediator: But you know that that is just an opinion, like any other opinion. But I'm sure he's an informed and knowledgeable person. The only way mediation can work is by both sides recognizing that the other guy isn't completely wrong. Maybe then we can start to reach agreement, maybe we can have nobody get hurt too much. If the judge decides either owes $492., one or the other gets hurt a lot. Is there give in any part of this thing?. . . .

(Source: Court Mediation Service, Portland, Maine)

(P)'s offer of the sworn statement is a moment of political resistance and indicates a conflict between conceptions of justice. The suppression of principle or issues that would challenge the process facilitate the movement toward consent. Another illustration of how legal norms and rights are replaced by consensus that does not necessarily flow from the desires or interests of the parties is indicated in the following exchange. The disputants are former roommates arguing about bills.

Mediator: So you're taking $5.00 out?

R: Right, the rest of it I will pay.

P: Am I being unreasonable?

Mediator: I don't know now, you both have a good point here. Neither one of you is completely right, but certainly neither one of you is completely wrong. Ah, why don't we trade-off one of these [bills] for the other? If you'd be willing to back down on the ticket, maybe she'd be willing to back down on the painting. You know, in that case I don't think either one of you is both completely wrong. (Source: Court Mediation Service, Portland, Maine)

It is the development of a nonredefinable problem by sequencing the activities of the participants in a certain way—narrowing, shifting attention from the problem to solutions and narrowing the range of solutions in such a way that disputants cannot review the problem itself, in relation to the solutions generated, that makes consensus as a form of hegemony possible and differentiates mediation from psychotherapy or education. It restricts rather than expands options. The process establishes an irreversible sequence of action so that disputants have no other recourse. Once they move from one point to the next, they normally do not reflect on or review where they have come from. The mediator's objective is to reach an agreement and adopt a solution—not to analyze the problem, examine the past, or define the issues. The content of solutions is not as important as that there be a solution arrived at in this process. From the point of view of some mediators, disputants' resistance to the principles of mediation is interpreted as being rigid or overly moralistic (Interview with mediator, Miami, Florida, 1979).

At the same time, no party is to consider what might be "just" as a possible solution to the original problem. It might only occur as coincidence. Thus, there is no rational agreement that a given problem *required* the particular solution reached. The agreement requires that the solution, whatever its content, be accepted, regardless of the original problem. The Crime and Justice Foundation manual observes that the mediator "should absolutely not voice an opinion to either party as to whose version of the facts s/he believes" (1980: 44). The mediator manual for the Commission on Community Relations, Landlord-Tenant Mediation Project in Denver provided these instructions to the parties which reveals how conflict is restructured and ordered toward consensus.

Choose your topics carefully and then stick to the issues. Spend very little time discussing the dispute. Stress the points that you agree upon. Instead of rehashing the original disagreement, use your energies on how the problem can be resolved. Think what you want to say before you start talking. Focus on neutral rather than negative wording, i.e.: "situation" rather than "problem," "misunderstanding" rather than "argument" (Martinson, 1981: A-1).

Mediators are not seeking to clarify issues but to clarify options and arrive at practical alternatives. As one mediator in Miami, Florida commented: "You can't spend too much time on truth—otherwise you won't get anywhere. The idea is to get a solution and not focus on details" (Interview, 1979).

In ordinary interaction when priorities are set, alternatives are listed and kept in reserve for possible reflection and later change. This is not the case here. Mediation is a thoroughly nondialectical process moving the parties away from the chance to rethink the situation. The skills and authority of the mediators, themselves evaluated according to cases resolved, play a role here. A project director of a program in California suggested that: "The problem is one of verbal influence. The mediators are very skilled at getting parties to agree—too skilled. This is what they're trained to do, but the agreement may not be the one the parties want" (Interview, 1980). Yet, ironically, the process appears unbounded, open and without rules; it can lead to any number of outcomes. The court has limited alternatives too. But in mediation those limits are concealed in a surrogate official process that is irreversible in its definition of the problem and movement toward solutions. Through this informal process, the issue shifts from justice to dispute resolution. People are thereby encourged to bring their problems to a highly institutionalized forum that restricts alternatives without appearing to do so. Consensus as a mode of resolution and as an ideology is thus partly established by presenting alternatives to compromise itself as impossible, unworkable, and, most importantly, uncivilized and irrational. One mediator commented, "Some people are more difficult. They resist mediation. I can't communicate with them" (Interview, 1979).

And this process of accommodation or narrowing the range of solutions, and the focus on a linear path toward solution, is the way in which the parties are driven toward treating all kinds of conflicts in the same way, as no different than any other. Thus we get a homogenization of conflict (Garofalo and Connelly, 1980b). As a study by the Vera Institute of Justice indicated, "in view of the highly individualized content of the mediation sessions, there was a surprising sameness to the agreements that emerged" (Davis et al., 1980: 48).

Accommodation also supports order-maintenance, as mediators—by training and in their mostly middle-class backgrounds—express social values that support the perspective of state power. The study by the Vera Institute also noted how mediators attempted to support social values such as kinship, reciprocity, and the need to avoid violence. "The mediation process simulates an idealized form of good social relations, and provides an example of how to break out of bad social behavior patterns" (Davis et al, 1980: 42, 43).

What are the implications of this process? The agreement to bargain from the outset is already a capitulation, a redefinition of the problem brought by disputants and a way of rationalizing conflict. To borrow Michael Burawoy's (1979) phrase, mediation "manufactures consent." The regulation of conflict by means of accommodation assumes consensus about the values underlying the social order, and this regulation diverts attention from substantive issues and principles in the larger social context. It is not just that facts are eliminated but that they are reconstructed. Discussing environmental disputes, P. Baldwin comments,

Dispute settlement should not become an end in itself, particularly when important environmental values are at stake. Not peace at any price, but sound environmental decisions must be the goal. . . . Conflict avoidance, or premature settlement may obscure the important issues, while protracted and difficult disputes may result in the most creative and lasting accomplishments (1978: 9).

Neutrality is not equivalent to refraining from explicitly taking sides, and values may be manifested in ways other than direct advocacy. Mediators bring with them their social class, ethnic heritage, and professional and political ideologies (Starr, 1981). Informality does not dispense with norms; they are only articulated less clearly. The unstated assumptions of a professionally trained cadre of middle-class mediators about what constitutes a reasonable claim, the proper use of force, or the content of justice may have a significant bearing on the outcome, particularly when the parties are predominantly poor, inner-city residents. Moreover, the rush to consensus obscures the positive need for conflict as the only effective means for resisting "political repression, racism, and sexism" (Abel, 1981: 249). The pretention to impartiality conceals the authority of the state and the presence of a bureaucratic authority. Just as workers become more dependent on capitalist organization of the work process, so informalism deprives community members of political competence by transferring power to nondemocratic agencies of the state.

As rights expand into opaque and technical areas such as the disclosure of finance charges in the consumer credit system and statutory prerequisites to rent an increase when rent control is in effect, the individual has a strong interest in enforcing the letter of the law. In an informal setting, such "technical" rules, which are designed with a larger regulatory purpose in mind, would probably be overlooked as irrelevent to the substance of a particular dispute (Rubinstein, 1976: 81).

There is no conception or examination of justice, rights, or norms, but only a soft bureaucratic procedure for redressing grievances or compensating injuries.

Such settlement through bargaining restricts the scope of inquiry and thereby reproduces the inequalities of power that enable a local business, for example, to engage in overcharging or otherwise to defraud the consumer without risking a sanction more serious than repayment. It can also produce results without raising challenges to established power. Mark Lazerson (1982) demonstrated, for example, that when Legal Services attorneys achieved some degree of success in obtaining delays and challenging law in landlord-tenant court in the Bronx, landlords sought to settle the cases in the halls, informally. When formal legality became effective for those normally without power, accommodation meant a quick result without challenge to landlord legal rights. In cases where consumers initiate action, accommodation can serve as a buffer against serious claims. The director of a program in Florida explained, in response to a question about the willingness of merchants to use mediation, "One reason that they [merchants] come here is so that it won't go any further" (Interview, 1979).

Settlement through consensus, moreover, is not likely to result in the articulation of general criteria applicable to injurious conduct in the future. The ideology of consensus conceals patterns of activity that extend beyond the immediate case. It eliminates the language of politics and obscures the clash of real interests. The result is political impotence.

This consensus process, however, is fraught with difficulties. Many disputants simply want to win and view their position as correct. "Compromise," according to one Florida-based mediator, "is conceived as a stalling tactic by some" (Interview, 1979). Achieving consensus is a subtle and delicate affair. Some disputants withdraw, express hositility toward mediators, or engage in behavior that may sabotage the process (Folberg and Taylor, 1984). Except for Christine Harrington (1980; 1985), who explored the need for incentives and threats to initiate the use of mediation to its conclusion, few researchers have systematically explored those who reject mediation outright as a possibility or detailed the problems experienced by those who failed to reach or sustain agreements. Because consent is artificially structured, the "order" it creates remains fragile. The absence of an authentic consensus and the striving to achieve a false unity is part of the potential undoing of NDR, and a way to reveal its ideological construction. The rush to consensus, even though it creates a language of order, does not contain an educative component related to an explicit conception of community. If it did move beyond discipline and order, toward creating real cohesion through broader discussion and analysis less controlled by mediators and those who plan mediation, then the institution could be transformed into a forum unbounded by the limited discourse of consensus. Without the mediator's pushing toward settlement and in other ways providing direction, the outcomes would be more uncertain, the process less routine, less filtered. While it is difficult to predict how disputants might work through conflicts differently, a less rationalized system might open spaces in which to examine the social and political sources of conflict, in order to make the connection between conflict and community problems. Just as people in relationships sometimes fear the expression of anger will destroy a relationship and so repress their feelings, mediation planners fear the full expression of conflict, distrusting disputants (and a larger public) to work through conflict in their own less organized way. Allowing people to do this would be an empowerment, a form of self-reliance without predefined rules. NDR would then be a vehicle for social reconstruction rather depoliticization. Dynamic community social life depends on diversity, on people creating their own history. It may be messy, disorderly, and incomplete. But people could make their own peace in their own way.

The Appearance of Everyday Life through an Administrative Procedure

For hegemony to work, domination must be experienced as natural, and universal, and the values of the dominant class internalized. At the same time, domination must be expressed through working class ideologies. Artificially creating an institution through a formal state apparatus which incorporates people's own cultural context would seem to be a formidable task. This is what NDR can do, and it represents an essential dimension of its hegemonic appeal and another means by which some people accept NDR as legitimate, even though it opposes an already traditional view of conflict resolution found in the formal judicial system. The staging rules, setting, rituals, and discourse of mediation present an appearance of everyday life, suggesting an absence of state power. The state is invisible in a face-to-face process. This face-to-face direct representation, not the inculcation of doctrine, will partially determine the success of NDR and its ideology.

Badges and uniforms are absent. The mediators present themselves as friendly, neutral, concerned, patient, respectful, and understanding (Cook et al., 1980). Yet mediators are typically strangers, in many cases trained professionals who are not of the same social class as disputants (Merry, 1979; Starr, 1981). They are neither the friends or the therapists of the disputants. A mediator in the Ft. Lauderdale program explained bluntly that, in mediation, "middle-class values dominate in contrast to working-class values. Sometimes both parties are treated like defendants because of their social status" (Interview, 1979). Mediation sessions are sometimes conducted in storefronts, and even in people's homes in special circumstances (Interview, Los Angeles, 1980). The project location itself, removed from the symbols of legal authority, suggests the absence of the state. "A neutral setting conveys an image of impartiality and accessibility . . . an official setting may reflect the coerciveness of the program" (Trzyna and Knab, 1978). Formal ceremony is absent. The language is nonlegal and commonsensical; disputants explain their version of events in their own time and words. The form of discourse relies on understandings of ordinary morality (Greason, 1980). Disputants engage in storytelling activity, directed toward a sympathetic listener, the mediator. A consequence of employing the discourse of everyday life in a process without law expands the power of the state. It permits a greater entry into people's private lives. In part, this is achieved by expanding the range of social interactions in the subject matter deemed actionable, as well as the remedies available. In many programs, case criteria for eligibility are broadly defined (Roehl and Cook, 1982). These programs, like juvenile diversion programs, handle cases concerned not only with violations of law but also with behavior identified as a social problem or a threat to community stability. The range of subject matter handled is extensive (Ray et al., 1986; Garofalo and Connelly, 1980a; McGillis, 1982). A substantial proportion of cases may represent new disputes rather than merely the diversion of controversies already in the courts (Shonholtz, 1984; Singer, 1979). But clearly most cases in many NDR forums would never have passed the charge stage (Alper and Nichols, 1981: 138). Informal procedures thus permit a wide variety of noncriminal but disapproved conduct to be subjected to scrutiny and even to sanctions. Everyone and everything potentially becomes a relevant subject for state intervention. In some court-based programs

there appear to be no formal limitations on the discretion of court clerks, prosecutors, judges, and others in determining which cases are suitable for referral to mediation, no formal limitations on whatever discretion the mediation staff has in accepting referrals, and no formal limitations on the discretion of community mediators in conducting their sessions (Snyder, 1978: 788).

Without the formal protections of due process—for example, open hearings and rules of evidence—disputants may enter the system when they would never be processed by the courts, or even by the police (Harrington, 1980).

Once in the system, mediation cases are almost never dismissed. A study by the Vera Institute of Justice evaluating a program that handles mostly criminal cases (Davis et al., 1980) indicates that "most cases referred to mediation would have been dismissed if they had instead been forwarded to court for prosecution" (iii). In this study, "only 28 percent of the control cases resulted in misdemeanor guilty pleas or in transfer of the complaint to the grand jury for felony indictment. . . . " (iii). Those that may hesitate to participate, especially in quasi-criminal cases, are pressured to participate (Davis, 1982). In some court-based programs, respondents sometimes receive letters on official stationery from the prosecutor's office. A program director in Florida commented that "an official document is a necessity, even though the program is voluntary. Otherwise they won't show" (Interview, 1979).

Unlike formal legal processes which usually occur after a serious breach of order and usually long after the precipitating event, informal processes emphasize immediacy of intervention and the prevention of future conflict (Cohen, 1985; Blum, 1980; Felstiner and Williams, 1978; Synder, 1978: 751). Many programs, for example, intervene before any agent or the parties file a formal complaint. Initiation of a complaint is easy and eligibility criteria are broad, unlike the criteria necessary for judicial action. Effective resolution is the objective, tempered by the "realization that legal rules constrain the capacity to handle the parties" (Educational and Psychological Development Corporation, 1978: 2). The earlier the intervention "the more likely it is to have significant impact on the behavior of the persons involved in the crisis" (Educational and Psychological Development Corporation: 8). Such behavioral specificity is less likely in a judicial proceeding, governed by fixed procedural rules. NDR is thus affirmative rather than reactive. It can expand the capacity of the courts to manage social life. As Frederick E. Snyder indicates, describing the comments of a judge in the Dorchester district which had a mediation project, without the presence of a mediation project, cases would "have merely been continued without a finding or would have ended with the defendant on probation. [No] resource coordinator would be on hand to monitor such cases and help steer the parties into honoring their commitments to one another" (1978: 775).

The discourse and interaction of the everyday reduces the appearance of the state and simultaneously expands the discretionary authority of its agents, thereby expanding state power. Discretion is inherent in the administrative form.

> [The administrative form of legalization] denies all class antagonism, appeals to general standards of harmony and public welfare, and pretends to focus on equity by emphasizing the unique circumstances of every case. . . . [it] legitimates virtually any administrative action or inaction. . . . It represents a return to unrestricted political power. . . . It delegalizes social relations by liberating direct power which law tries to formalize (Reifner, 1982: 84).

Informality is more flexible than judicial proceedings because it rejects principles that apply to all in order to realize some abstract public good. Supplementing the rule of law with informality can thus expand the state.

> The development of state-regulated, monopoly capitalism has also witnessed the erosion of the rule of law and the emergence of less formalistic, more instrumentalist and technocratic modes of social and political control. The law as universal political equivalent gradually gives way to a series of relatively *ad hoc techniques* which, by their very nature, recognize specific interests and specific social origins. . . . Technocratic modes of social control imply a certain re-emergence of the content and quality from which the legal form abstracts (Balbus, 1977: 586).

Informalism also expands state power by blurring the distinction between public and private power through an open-ended process that emphasizes, in its objectives, problem solving rather than interpreting a legal rule. In this sense, it is policy-oriented, purposive, and geared toward direct, substantive intervention.

In most neighborhood mediation programs there is no public record, no open hearings, no recognized rights, and no formal rules of evidence (Snyder, 1979). No one records the experience for future reference or appeal as in a trial court. Only the parties may be present, although some programs do allow friends or witnesses. Legal rights embodied in judicial precedent or constitutional law do not apply. No subject is specifically excluded or

included. All comments are generally welcome because the mediator does not judge but facilitates the movement toward a solution.
   The symbols of the state and direct coerciveness disappear. The
location is typically an informal setting, without the accoutre-
ments and images of the court. The new symbolic language emphasizes civil, everyday terms rather than legal terms (e.g., respondent not defendant, mediator not judge, problem not deviance).
The Crime and Justice Foundation in Massachusetts stresses the
pleasantries of the introductory remarks and the nature of mediator manipulation.

Opening remarks must be presented in a cordial manner that encourages
the disputants to relax and let down their defenses.

[The] mediator attempts to prompt each party to view his/her position
in a flexible manner, as well as to see the desirability of a settlement.
Since both language and mannerisms contribute toward making the disputants feel at ease and creating a congenial, informal atmosphere, the
mediators must greet their guests warmly and shake hands all around
(1980: 36, 12).

   Whereas in the courtroom the judge imposes decisions and
manages cases through agreed upon rules, mediators use the discretion that comes with informality to invade and manipulate the
psyches of disputants in order to achieve a solution. For example,
here is a written instruction to disputants about how to behave in
order for mediation to work.

BE CALM. Do not attempt to speak with the other party until you are
calm enough to carry on a conversation without shouting, crying, or
getting angry. Don't let the other party provoke you into an argument.
If the other party starts yelling or behaving in an unreasonable manner,
continue to be calm. You may have to leave and arrange to meet at another time, but if you allow the conversation to breakdown into a shouting match, you will probably lose your chance to work out the dispute
between the two of you (Martinson, 1981: A-1).

   The mediator can uncover information without concern for rules
of evidence or facts. As I have stressed, by probing parties about
their feelings and attitudes, and encouraging them to express their
feelings, mediation operates as a subtle form of policing that tran-

scends traditional state activity in managing illegal behavior or even bureaucratic rule violations. The state can thereby provide specialized detailed interventions or treatment to deal with almost any form of social disruption or disagreeable behavior. The state thus intensifies its surveillance of civil society.

In contrast to the courts, mediation . . . is concerned with uncovering the dynamic of the interpersonal problems from which the incident arose. While the initial focus of a mediation session may be the incident, the mediator guides the disputing parties toward an agreement which is intended to minimize future conflict rather than apportion guilt and sanctions. Based on the assumption that there is an underlying problem, a mediator attempts to understand and to solve the dispute from which the incident arose. Thus, both the complainant and the defendant are encouraged to present their sides of the story and to propose solutions acceptable from their respective viewpoints (Davis et al., 1980: 40).

Few limits are imposed on the issues investigated if discussion helps disputants reach agreement. Intake counselors usually solicit much diagnostic information from participants before the hearing. Within the mediation session, many programs encourage disputants to "tell their stories," ventilate their feelings, and otherwise reveal details about their personal lives. According to A. L. Greason, a psychologist and mediator in a small claims court in Maine, "the mediator can let people speak emotionally and irrelevantly, even shout obscenities if necessary. This at least clears the air and convinces people that they are being heard—that what is important to them is being listened to" (1980: 578). The purpose is not to punish or reprimand but rather to understand the roots of the conflict. In doing so, mediation deals with the totality of the individual (e.g., character, behavior, feelings, history) and not merely the situation. Courts may do this too. But in mediation the emphasis on the social rather than the legal aspect of conflict is a central characteristic (Merry and Silbey, 1984). Such therapeutic openness magnifies the extent to which the state can oversee the lives of disputants, without their experiencing that oversight as control. Their deepest emotions and most personal problems become part of the process of conflict resolution. This intervention itself is regulation, a form of policing, regardless of its effect

on the outcome (Feeley, 1980). Why? It is a self-deceptive cathar-
sis induced and organized by the mediator as a means to contain
"anti-productive" emotions and manage the parties. Such management is not the rationale a friend or even a psychotherapist
would use in having someone reveal themselves. The nature of
the interactions or bond with the mediator is not one of mutual
caring or trust. This reminder to mediators gives some indication
of the distinction:

LET THEM VENT: A lot of the time, the problem is simply that no
one will listen to their frustrations with their tenant/landlord. Once they
get it "off their chests" they are better able to get down to business.
(Martinson, 1981: A-14).

These programs can also be understood to manage disputants'
lives in the requirements stipulated in the agreements. The content
of many agreements often contains detailed references to changes
in behavior or attitude that would ordinarily appear beyond the
purview of the state. The following summary of cases excerpted
from a program brochure in St. Petersburg, Florida offers an indication.

Twelve year old Mike and 11 year old Bob live next door to 80 year
old Mrs. Croff. . . .The boys play in their back yard, and whenever their
ball or frisbee comes into Mrs. Croff's yard she runs out and takes the
toy and keeps it. The boys try to jump over the fence to get the toy and
when Mrs. Croff sees the boys do this, she calls the police. The boys'
mother and Mrs. Croff have had arguments and the boys' mother told
Mrs. Croff to "_____ off". Mrs. Croff thinks this woman should be
put in jail for such awful language.
RESOLUTION
    A hearing was held and Mrs. Croff agreed that she would not keep the
kids' toys; rather will throw them back over the fence. She agreed not to
call the police unless she talked first with the mother. The mother agreed
she would not swear at Mrs. Croff. . . .So far, no more trouble.

Georgia Smith is beaten every Friday by her husband Fred because he
spends a good portion of his paycheck on booze. The police are [often]
called. . . .Mrs. Smith wants to prosecute each time, but never appears
for a State Attorney investigation. Finally, an officer refers her to C.D.S.

RESOLUTION

The couple comes to a hearing and talks to a psychologist. Mr. Smith agrees to come home after work each Friday and Mrs Smith . . . picks up the paycheck weekly. They agree to go to family counseling. Mr. Smith agrees to attend AA. So far, no more trouble.

Mr. Swinger and Mrs. Straight have been neighbors for about a year. Mr. Swinger keeps late hours, plays his stereo rather loudly until 1:00 A.M. and has an assortment of women friends who sometimes visit Mr. Swinger. . . .Mrs. Straight has to get up at 6:00 A.M. to go to work, . . . and she is used to living in a "nice, respectable neighborhood." After answering three noise nuisance calls in two weeks, the police referred both parties to C.D.S

RESOLUTION

At the hearing, Mr. Swinger agreed to turn his music down promptly at 10:30 P.M., so Mrs. Straight can go to sleep. Mr. Swinger further agreed to ask his friends not to make excessive noise outside. Mrs. Straight agreed to call Mr. Swinger instead of the police if there is any further problem. So far, no problems (Citizen Dispute Settlement Program, St. Petersburg, Florida, 1979).

These cases all involve a contract to refrain from action or to behave in a certain way under specified conditions. While the solutions appear rational, they suggest a subtle intrusion into people's lives. The parties may or may not have been able to work their problems to a similar conclusion. But such detailed agreements, overseen by the state, represent a sanction and style of self-policing, apart from whether there may be a legal violation of privacy (Harrington, 1985). Disputants will monitor each other in order to determine if a violation of agreement occurs. The disputants in these cases have experienced the hegemony of the state in agreeing to accept the solutions. Moreover, noting the second case where Mr. Smith beats his wife, women's groups have argued that wifebeating should generally not be handled as a private matter and that women should prosecute these types of cases (Tolchin, 1985). At a minimum, such abuse may require that it be registered with a public agency. The first case about the boys and their toys is a good example of how everyone may become a subject for corrective state intervention. It is precisely the innocuous quality of the solution—simple, satisfying, minimal police involvement—that suggests how the state can interfere in ordinary social life, if its images and symbols connect with expectations about behavior.

Equally important, the mediator, in seeking a successful outcome, may subtly pressure disputants by hinting at the possible negative consequences of failure—the threat of return to court or channeling them toward an agreement (Snyder, 1978; Garofalo and Connelly, 1980b). Violation of the agreement can result in the initiation or renewal of prosecution (Davis et al., 1980).

Just as workers are monitored in the workplace (Edwards, 1979), offenders supervised by probation officers (Cohen, 1979), so parties in the neighborhood dispute resolution forum may find their lives exposed to continuing scrutiny. The form of regulation may be less overt and appear less obtrusive than in other institutions, but it still reflects a restructuring of control from a focus on limited action that violates specific norms to a concern with behaviors, habits, attitudes, and the defiance of bureaucratic authority.

Informalism not only conceals the exercise of state power but presents the appearance of a contraction of state power when such power merely takes another form (Santos, 1982). In this way, NDR seemingly represents a response to the impasse resulting from the boundedness of the judicial system as a tool for social interventions. However, although the opportunity for precision and flexibility increases, there are contradictions.

By bringing new cases into the judicial system that would not have entered it (as opposed to diverting old cases), the state expands its managerial requirements yet still may not have the capacity to manage what enters its purview. Discretion is political. By expanding discretion the potential for resistance increases since, without fixed rules, procedures may come to be questioned, ignored, or undermined. People's desire for real control of their disputes, given a seemingly open-ended system, constitutes the basis for a challenge to formalized dispute resolution. The initial question for citizens is: do we really need professional mediators with nationally-based models telling us how to resolve our conflicts?

At another level, the discourse of everyday life makes the process indeterminate with a potential for creativity that suggests alternatives to the process itself. The unreliability and unpredictability of the everyday can lead back to a further attempt at rationalization and administrative control. Or it can lead to a more democratic process and a collective public, grounded in its own discourse, determined to establish autonomy from the bottom up.

Examples of how this could happen may be seen in a variety of community movements whereby people reject the bureaucratic authority of experts, planners, and professionals and take charge of decision making. On nuclear power and toxic waste issues, citizens in many communities find they can learn the questions and how to use experts while controlling the fundamental political decisions. On a more regular basis, models of activist citizen participation can be found in Peoples' Councils or Citizen Utility Boards, where the state funds consumer representatives to intervene before public bodies.

NDR seems to be an arena that does not require national models and experts defining how community and interpersonal conflict ought to be handled. People can question its principles and establish their own rules. As they realize the dispensability of lawyers, the need for any state professionals to guide dispute resolution processes may be questioned.

Conclusion

The revitalization of neighborhood dispute resolution forums is a phase in an ongoing restructuring and expansion of the capitalist state. A central feature in the structuring concerns the continued blurring between state and civil society such that the state does not appear to be the state but rather part of the landscape of community social life. One result is a shift in the nature of ideological domination in shaping human relationships. Practices and symbols within the core social institutions of everyday life colonize public space in new ways that permit NDR to appear as something other than its surface features indicate. NDR's hegemonic qualities rely heavily on commitment to and participation in its definition of order as a means for social regulation. At the same time, given its contradictions and paradoxes, NDR contains elements with a liberatory potential, making it highly unstable, subject to transformation.

I have sought to show why fully understanding NDR requires an exploration of its relation to the peculiar, ever-changing demand for order in captialist society, under given historical conditions, rather than simply as a modern, homespun means for dispute resolution. Embedded within its structure, rules, processes, and rituals is a particular conception of social and political relations, based on the organization of power in a capitalist society. This conception bears little relation to people's lived experience. Conventional analyses have sought to explain NDR by looking for causes; by examining its observable processes at face value; and by using legal concepts and psychological categories, and standard program evaluation practices. But NDR cannot be evaluated according to technocratic criteria—such as caseloads or disputant surveys. Nor can we understand it by exploring the motivations of planners or practitioners, beliefs about new philosophical solutions to conflict, deficiencies in the judicial system, or a general demand for alternatives by a public hostile to the courts. Most importantly, it cannot be understood by a universal need to suppress social conflict. We need to ask: Whose agenda is NDR? Whose rules of organization define it?

By situating it in a theory of crisis and the state within an anarchic corporate capitalist economy, NDR can be named as a system for social crisis management, as a governing mechanism rather than an "alternative" or "nonlegal" phenomenon for dispensing justice. It remains a form of law, structured in an unconventional way, and therefore should not even be thought of as nonlegal in any pure sense. It is part of the ideological ensemble of law, although it appears to be external to law. One may refer to it as nonlegal only in that it offers particular controls rather than general responses. But the institution as a whole is general, and applied for all conditions and conflicts. Political containment and administrative surveillance define its most critical unstated objectives, in contrast with community justice or community empowerment. It shares many characteristics of phenomena like little city halls, neighborhood advisory councils, planning boards, and other corporate-developed institutions oriented toward absorbing discontent by civilizing and rationalizing conflict.

The crisis of order that could result in NDR concerns the growing disruptions to the circuits of capital (production-exchange-consumption) in an increasingly unstructured, incoherent environment, lacking legitimate authority, norms, and consistent ideology. Because capital permeates every sphere of social life, instability may occur at each location in the social order that it touches. The infrastructural environment—the city—is increasingly important, intricate, and fragile. It is what makes labor possible because labor is produced through city life.

Capital expansion recomposes the working class as a society of production within cities. Labor bearing labor power is itself a social infrastructre—not a collection of individuals. Impairments to this infrastructure are exacerbated because there is no control over investment. People cannot rely on living in stable communities as a result of disinvestment and concessions which create a mobile, impoverished workforce with minimal attachments. Yet labor's availability for capital depends on skills, technology, and people's settled, stable connections with each other in communities. These communities must be maintained. Disinvestment undermines mediating institutions such as unions and families. In this all-encompassing interdependent environment, less room exists for waste and disruption. Managing consumer demand, employment levels, and capital mobility means that private activity and formerly nontreatable behavior become a public concern. More than disorder arising from reductions in public services, unbridled global capital everywhere creates resistances and undermines civil authority, so that the crisis for capital is struggle rather than social disintegration per se. The struggle intensifies to the extent that the political system is unwilling or unable to meet demands for claims ordinarily processed through its institutions.

But as social space is transformed, the dynamic for hegemony and control shift. Traditional symbols lose their connection to any basis in reality. With the destruction of local political systems and their replacement by corporate control, a new kind of policy making occurs in the city, whereby elected, accountable governments lose much of their formal power to make policy. With the increasing consolidation of captial, policy is subject to coordination among banks and institutions above the political system. More than stabilizing the labor force and extracting the surplus, political control itself is required to manage this total environment in ways limited by the rule of law or conventional authority. At the same time, workers still strive to meet subsistence needs and emancipate themselves from capitalist prerogatives, leading to new oppositional cultures. The exhaustion of traditional remedies, such as courts, police, family, church, welfare, political machines, or indeed any centralized apparatus, and more indeterminate disruptive situations produces other options, NDR among them.

NDR thus arises in this chaos as a means to order settlements, reinforcing a sense of stability while that stability is continually undermined. The specific kind of social order required for capitalist expansion does not occur automatically; it must be created artificially, because people cannot be anchored to a social system on the basis of market principles, the law of value, or efficiency principles. Law may justify power but it cannot create community. There must be shared norms. Yet no criteria for judging society exist—only rules. Neither science, religion, or the work ethic can create community. Nor can the enchantment of consumption or other diversions create a social fabric free of rupture, chaos, dislocation, and unpredictable conflict at a time when neighborhoods are disintegrating in many places, marginalizing great sectors of the population. Capital expansion also requires active consent and mobilization of support in a Gramscian sense, not simply passive conformity. Dynamic innovation that leads to growth demands freely circulating labor and creativity, but not democratic challenges to capitalist prerogatives.

New types of political domination, like NDR, occur in these spaces, under these conditions, not necessarily connected in appearance to any formal state apparatus or bureaucratic authority. The social and private spaces have formerly been marginal and usually protected from state interference. NDR, a form of self-policing, emerges as a supplement to existing institutions at the local level as a means for administering conflict. The mechanisms for social control that were once transferred to the formal state are now transferred back to the community in a revised form, embedded in the community but alien to it.

If NDR survives as presently constituted through the state, a number of potential dangers can be summarized. First, NDR could promote the further destruction of public life in the way it desocializes conflicts and transforms or conceals public issues in a private process. This fragmenting, decentering of the collective may destroy indigenous forms of justice, leading to further deterioration in neighborhood cohesion, community responsibility, and social movements. Citizens are given mediation by powerful forces. It is not developed through a grassroots process whereby people use their own knowledge. NDR imposes a logic and rhetoric of community trust, mutual obligation, and community peace making without any organic community. NDR thus individualizes rather than unites people in their common concerns. Real community is politics. Conflict resolution could become a service leading to political impotence. Political debate and advocacy could atrophy within the current NDR models, to the extent that values remain unquestioned and mediation colonizes thought about conflict, particularly the idea that there is too much conflict in society and mediation is the solution. Conflict may suggest inequality or discrimination, or unmet needs requiring new law or dramatic institutional change. Maybe protest and civil disobedience are necessary to rectify inequalities. To the extent that people use NDR, they may rely less on working-class and other types of organizations. The rent strike, for example, is a form of working-class organization. At the same time, NDR, in its direct surveilling of everyday life, is an extension and intensification of state power in a way that Bertram Gross called "friendly fascism." Using a newly trained class of professional mediators, NDR rhetoric stresses getting to the underlying roots of conflict—meaning psychological or personal, not social, roots. Ironically, the disputants act out their conflict, enervating themselves, but do not necessarily come to an emotional understanding. This acting out or release through storytelling is an example of how domination functions in a process. The danger involves the way people are seduced in a process not their own. The flexible, friendly, seemingly voluntary face-to-face process, unconnected to visible rules or rights in an atmosphere indistinguishable from the everyday is indeed engaging. Yet the purpose is to cool-out disputants, not to assist them in making valid claims.

SPECULATIONS, PROSPECTS, FUTURES: THE NEGATIVE

NDR as a hegemonic state institution is likely to change direction regardless of whether the three hundred–odd programs and countless procedures continue. There are two intertwined types of reasons, apart from recognizing that historical conditions will change. One concerns its contradictions that destroy its own definition of itself. The other concerns resistances.

NDR is not a rational solution to the social order, nor does it bear any relation to traditional notions about justice. The contradiction between conflict management and social justice cannot be solved in its framework. It applies an idea of Jeffersonian democracy, popular sovereignty, and self-management within a system designed to enhance the corporate state, not community or justice. Whether such rhetoric can be sustained with the increasing size of governing units, the polarization and inequities among social classes, and the increasing mobility and the expansion of discord is questionable. NDR assumes universal values at work in resolving conflicts. But it cannot solve the collective problems that people experience because its primary role is order-maintenance. Ironically, even if NDR could create community, it would be undesirable from the point of view of corporate capital. Collective unity in urban populations may lead to confrontation politics creating a solidarity resisting capitalist exploitation. NDR's effect is to demobilize and discourage collective action that could establish community. So its managerial aims inherent in its political construction always conflict with its pretentions to be community-oriented. Moreover, the problems that people bring to NDR are social not individual, and the outside world cannot be suspended.

Because NDR is technocratic, without substantive norms, it cannot relate fully to people's experiences, however much it uses the language and images of everyday life. The absence of unity and purpose in American society, coupled with the expansion of leisure, desire, and unpredictability in daily life, limit the state's capacity to manage social life in specific ways. As political conflict expands under the conditions of a declining domestic economy and an interdependent world economy, the institutionalization of conflict through compromise and consent may prove especially difficult.

These dispute resolution forums, informal and highly reliant on trained personnel, offer even less accountability to the public than do the courts. The rationalization demanded from them by the state—for routinization, for permanent records, and so forth—is imperfect. It is an institution without controls, and therefore may not provide the kind of managerial predictability and order required by a corporatist economy.

As NDR becomes institutionalized, the standardization or rationalization of its procedures may also limit its hegemonic capacities. Ossification could result from the capture of some forums by professionals who may drift down unpredictable paths. Moreover, to the extent that citizen users demand protections such as rights of appeal, confidentiality, the presence of attorneys, and other rights associated with the formal system, particularly as the process extends into new subject matter, NDR may lose the special qualities and appeal that define it and reinforce its effectiveness. At the same time as local administration fades, supplemented by NDR-like institutions, countertendencies are at work. Increasingly, for example, we now find more bureaucratic apparatuses operating directly through corporations or large institutions such as schools with their own judicial systems or grievance processes. Attention will be necessary to those conditions which suggest a collapse or restructuring of NDR.

People also resist NDR. They resist not only because NDR uses artificial rules and a false concept of participation, but because it is inherently exploitive, without any connection to social justice or the integrity of disputants. It is an alien state institution which presents itself as belonging to the community. Resistance is manifested in the refusal to participate and accept mediation's premises for handling conflict. In the process, people sometimes unwittingly challenge the premises by emphasizing right and wrong, arguing about justice or ethics rather than seeking settlement, and expressing distrust toward the mediators. They also sometimes violate the rules as they go through a mediation by interrupting each other or, at a future time, violate the agreement. Mediators cannot fully control how people finally interpret what they experience. But the future is open-ended. Every instance of ideological control produces an opening, a possibility.

SPECULATIONS: POSSIBILITIES AND A MODEL

Every moment of domination suggests a space for opposition and liberation, so that we need not be completely bounded in envisioning future directions or the possibility for challenge through extralegal means. If struggle propels social change, then a progressive conception of NDR is conceivable. Because there can be no final solution to the problem of order under capitalism, this potential always exists. Movement for change is not so easily tamed. These alien, unaccountable institutions are sold to the public as voluntary, participatory, and responsive. People may begin to act on those premises, unencumbered by any deeply felt commitment to administrative rules but given new expectations.

Questioning both conventional legality and NDR's current construction might lead to more democratic or popular systems of justice with less structure, less specialized knowledge, and less abstract contract-like relations (see, for example, Issacman and Issacman, 1982; Santos, 1982; Shonholtz, 1984). The mobilization of law could be open, public, nonprofessional, and independent, emphasizing social reconstruction and not merely reducing the irritations of everyday life. The sources of conflict could be interpreted within a broad social context—unemployment, poor housing, property relations—and handled by popularly elected agents who aggregate similar complaints (see Reifner, 1982).

Maureen Cain (1984) has outlined some elements for a popular collective restructuring of local justice. The clients of a revitalized community-based justice (meaning a process organized and managed by its users to meet their collective needs) would be interpreted as a collective subject on each side, not individuals. Such a collective subject could consider transforming the conditions of existence. Problems would be generalized to identify their class basis in an openly political manner. Similar complaints/conflicts could thereby be aggregated (see Reifner, 1982). The system would be purposively understood as class-related, committed to change, and not limited to a particular model. The staff would be popularly elected and accountable to the class they work for, making internal decisions on a democratic basis. The rules would be public, flexible, and derived from ethical and political theory and principles of social justice. A broad social context helps to identify the source of social conflict in unemployment, poor housing, and the conditions of work. In this model, people constitute themselves differently.

Whatever a revitalized, collective, democratic justice system might look like, the constraints in law and society that engender NDR will not disappear. The current NDR phase involves issues beyond justice without law. It concerns whether social decision making without politics and the management of social life without the appearance of the state can be progressively transformed.

NDR is as unpredictable as the social environment it seeks to rationalize. Its contradictions demonstrate its instability and susceptibility to challenge. Recapturing justice from the state will require dramatic changes. But the struggle for freedom and autonomy against capitalist power occurs wherever its forms emerge. To the extent that NDR undermines traditional civil authority and neighborhood organization, it creates a threat as well as an opportunity. NDR forums represent, at the same time, a way of channeling the energy of grassroots activists and a potential to mobilize for progressive change.

Bibliography

Aaronson, David E., Bert H. Hoff, Peter Jaszi, Nicholas N. Kittrie, and David Saari (1977) *The New Justice: Alternatives to Conventional Criminal Adjudication.* Washington, D.C.: National Institute of Law Enforcement and Criminal Justice.

Abel, Richard L. (1981) "Conservative Conflict and the Reproduction of Capitalism: The Role of Informal Justice," 9 *International Journal of the Sociology of Law* 245.

Abel, Richard L., ed. (1982a) *The Politics of Informal Justice*, 2 vols. New York: Academic Press.

Abel, Richard L., (1982b) "The Contradictions of Informal Justice," in Richard L. Abel, ed., *The Politics of Informal Justice, Volume 1: The American Experience.* New York: Academic Press.

Ad Hoc Panel on Dispute Resolution and Public Policy (1984) *Paths to Justice.* Washington, D.C.: U.S. Department of Justice and the National Institute for Dispute Resolution.

Agger, Simona Ganassi (1979) *Urban Self-Management: Planning for a New Society.* White Plains, N.Y.: M. E. Sharpe.

Agnew, J. A. (1981) "Home Ownership and the Capitalist Social Order," in Michael Dear and Allen J. Scott, eds., *Urbanization and Urban Planning in Capitalist Society.* London: Methuen.

Albany Dispute Mediation Program (1980) *Brochure.* Albany, N.Y.

Alcaly, Roger (1975) "The Relevance of Marxian Crisis Theory," in David Mermelstein, ed., *The Economic Crisis Reader.* New York: Vintage.

Allen, Francis A. (1964) *The Borderland of Criminal Justice.* Chicago: University of Chicago Press.

Alper, Benedict S., and Lawrence T. Nichols (1981) *Beyond the Courtroom: Programs in Community Justice and Conflict Resolution.* Lexington, Mass.: Lexington Books.

Althusser, Louis (1971) "Ideology and Ideological State Apparatuses," in Louis Althusser, ed., *Lenin and Philosophy and Other Essays.* New York: Monthly Review Press.

American Bar Association (1976) *Report of Pound Conference Follow-Up Task Force.* Chicago: American Bar Association.

Aronowitz, Stanley (1971) "Law, The Breakdown of Order and Revolution," in Robert Lefcourt, ed., *Law Against the People.* New York: Vintage.

Aronowitz, Stanley (1973) *False Promises.* New York: McGraw Hill.

Aronowitz, Stanley (1978) "Marx, Braverman, and the Logic of Capital," 8 *The Insurgent Sociologist* 126.

Aronowitz, Stanley (1981) *The Crisis in Historical Materialism.* South Hadley, Mass.: J. F. Bergin.

Aronowitz, Stanley (1985) "Why Work?" 12 *Social Text* 19.

Auerbach, Jerold S. (1983) *Justice Without Law: Resolving Disputes Without Lawyers.* New York: Oxford University Press.

Badcock, Blair (1984) *Unfairly Structured Cities.* Oxford, England: Basil-Blackwell.

Balbus, Issac (1976) "The Concept of Interest in Pluralist and Marxian Analysis," in Ira Katznelson et al., eds., *The Politics and Society Reader.* New York: David McKay.

Balbus, Issac (1977) "Commodity Form and Legal Form: An Essay on the 'Relative Autonomy' of the Law," 11 *Law and Society Review* 571.

Baldus, B. (1977) "Social Control in Capitalist Societies: An Examination of the 'Problem of Order,' " 2(3) *Canadian Journal of Sociology* 247–62.

Baldwin, P., ed. (1978) *Environmental Mediation: An Effective Alternative?* A report of a conference conducted in Reston, Virginia, January 11–13. Palo Alto, Calif.: RESOLVE.

Barlow, Andrew (1984) "In Defense of Litigation," 10(2) *Bar Leader* 17.

Baskin, Deborah (1984) "The People Next Door?: Community and Mediation in the United States." Ph.D. diss., University of Pennsylvania.

Berkson, Larry, and Susan Carbon (1978) *Court Unification: History, Politics, and Implementation.* Washington, D.C.: National Institute of Law Enforcement and Criminal Justice.

Bierne, Piers (1979) "Empiricism and the Critique of Marxism on Law and Crime," 26(4) *Social Problems* 373.

Binns, P. (1980) "Law and Marxism," 10 *Capital and Class* 100.

Block, Fred, and Larry Hirshhorn (1979) "New Productive Forces and the Contradictions of Contemporary Capitalism: A Post-Industrial Perspective," 7 *Theory and Society* 363.

Bluestone, Barry, and Bennett Harrison (1980) *Capital and Communities.* Washington, D.C.: The Progressive Alliance.

Blum, Martin S. (1980) *Citizen Dispute Settlement Project, The Municipal Court of Seattle: Quarterly Progress Report.* Seattle, Wash.: Municipal Court of Seattle (April).

Bookchin, Murray (1973) *The Limits of the City.* New York: Harper and Row.

Bowles, Samuel, and Herbert Gintis (1976) *Schooling in Capitalist America.* New York: Basic Books.

Bowles, Samuel, and Herbert Gintis (1982) "The Crisis of Liberal Democratic Capitalism: The Case of the United States," 11(1) *Politics and Society* 51.

Boyte, Harry (1979) "A Democratic Awakening," 10 *Social Policy* 8.

Boyte, Harry (1980) *The Backyard Revolution: Understanding the New Citizen Movement.* Philadelphia: Temple University Press.

Brady, James P. (1981) "Towards A Popular Justice in the United States: The Dialectics of Community Action," 5 *Contemporary Crises* 155.

Brady, James P. (1981) "Sorting Out The Exile's Confusion: Or Dialogue on Popular Justice," 5 *Contemporary Crises* 31.

Braverman, Harry (1974) *Labor and Monopoly Capital.* New York: Monthly Review Press.

Brenkman, John (1979) "Mass Media: From Collective Experience To the Culture of Privatization" 1 *Social Text* 94.

Brenkman, John (1983) "Theses On Cultural Marxism," 7 *Social Text* 19.

Brown, E. Richard (1979) *Rockefeller Medicine Men: Medicine and Capitalism in America.* Berkeley: University of California Press.

Buci-Glucksmann, Christine (1982) "Hegemony and Consent," in Anne Showstack Sassoon, ed., *Approaches To Gramsci.* London: Writers and Readers.

Buckle, Leonard G., and Suzann R. Thomas-Buckle (1981) "Self-Help Justice: Dispute Processing in Urban American Neighborhoods." Paper presented to the Law & Society Association annual meeting, Amherst, Massachusetts, June 1980.

Buckle, Leonard G., and Suzann R. Thomas-Buckle (1982) "Doing Unto Others: Dispute and Dispute Processing in an Urban American Neighborhood," in Roman Tomasic and Malcolm Feeley, eds., *Neighborhood Justice: Assessment of an Emerging Idea.* New York: Longman.

Budnitz, Mark (1977) "Consumer Dispute Resolution Forums," 13(12) *Trial* 45 (December).

Burawoy, Michael (1979) *Manufacturing Consent: Changes in the Labor Process Under Monopoly Capitalism.* Chicago: University of Chicago Press.

Burawoy, Michael (1981) "Terrains of Contest: Factory and State Under Capitalism and Socialism," 11(58) *Socialist Review* 83 (July-August).

Burger, Warren E. (1976) "Agenda for 2000 A.D.—A Need for Systematic Anticipation," 70 *Federal Rules Decisions* 83.

Cain, Maureen (1984) "Beyond Informal Justice." Working Paper no. 129. Florence, Italy: European University Institute.

Cain, Maureen, and Alan Hunt, eds. (1979) *Marx and Engels on Law.* New York: Academic Press.

Cain, Maureen, and Kalman Kulcsar (1982) "Thinking Disputes: An Essay on the Origins of the Dispute Industry," 16(3) *Law & Society Review* 375.

Cappelletti, Mauro, and Bryant Garth, eds. (1978) *Access To Justice: A World Survey*, Volume 1. Alpen aan den Rijn, Netherlands: Sitjhoff and Noordhoff.

Carnoy, Martin and Derek Shearer (1980) *Economic Democracy.* White Plains, New York: M. E. Sharpe.

Castells, Manuel (1976) "The Wild City," 4/5 *Kapitalistate* 2.

Center for Dispute Resolution, Denver, Colorado (1980) *Newletter* (April).

Chu, Franklin, and Sharland Trotter (1974) *The Madness Establishment.* New York: Grossman.

Cincinnati Institute of Justice (1984) *Reports on the Cleveland Prosecutor's Mediation Program.* Cincinnati, Ohio.

Citizen Dispute Settlement Program (1979) *Brochure.* St. Petersburg, Florida.

Citizen Dispute Settlement Program (1979) *Guidelines For Conducting A Successful Program.* Fort Lauderdale, Florida.

Clarke, Dean H. (1978) "Marxism, Justice, and the Justice Model," 2 *Contemporary Crises* 27.

Clarke, Simon (1983) "State, Class Struggle and the Reproduction of Capital," 10/11 *Kapitalistate* 113.

Cockburn, Cynthia (1977) *The Local State: Management of Cities and People.* London: Pluto Press.

Cohen, Stanley (1979) "The Punitive City: Notes on the Dispersal of Social Control," 3(4) *Contemporary Crises* 339.

Cohen, Stanley (1985) *Visions of Social Control.* Cambridge, England: Polity Press.

Committee for Economic Development (1980) *The Negotiated Investment Strategy: A Review of the Concept and Its Implications for Revitalizing Cities.* A report of the Subcommittee on Revitalizing America's Cities of the Committee for Economic Development. New York: Charles F. Kettering Foundation.

Community Board Program (1981) *The Community Board Center for Policy and Training: A Funding Proposal to Implement a Center to Support and Sustain Neighborhood Conflict Resolution Forums.* San Francisco: The Community Board Program.

Compa, Lance (1982) "The Dangers of Worker Control," 235(10) *The Nation* 300 (October 2).

Connelly, William (1981) "The Politics of Reindustrialization," 1(3) *Democracy* 9.

Conner, John T., and Milton Mapes, Jr. (1979) "Campaign Underway for National Peace Academy," *Newscope* 31.

Conner, Ross F., and Ray Surette (1977) *The Citizen Dispute Settlement Program: Resolving Disputes Outside the Courts—Orlando, Florida.* Chicago: American Bar Association.

Cook, Royer F., Janice A. Roehl, and David I. Sheppard (1980) *Neighborhood Justice Field Test—Final Evaluation Report.* Washington, D.C.: American Bar Association.

Coulson, Robert (1984) *Professional Mediation of Civil Disputes.* New York: American Arbitration Association.

Cox, Kevin R. (1981) "Capitalism and Conflict Around the Communal Living Space," in Michael Dear and Allen J. Scott, eds., *Urbanization and Urban Planning in Capitalist Society.* London: Methuen.

Cree, Thomas (1979) *Polk County Neighborhood Mediation Project, Polk County Attorney's Office: First Year Evaluation.* Des Moines, Iowa: Bureau of Governmental Research, Drake University.

Crime and Justice Foundation (1979) "A Look at Mediation in Massachusetts," 3(3) *Perspective* 3.

Crime and Justice Foundation (1980) *Mediation Training Manual.* Boston: Crime and Justice Foundation.

Criminal Justice Newsletter (1978) "A New National Judicial Planning Association." Hackensack, N. J.: National Council on Crime and Delinquency (May 22).

Cummings, Laird, and Joan Greenbaum (1978) "The Struggle Over Productivity: Workers, Management, and Technology," in Economics Education Project, Union for Radical Political Economics, ed., *U.S. Capitalism in Crisis.* New York: Union for Radical Political Economics.

Currie, Elliot (1985) *Crime and Community: Understanding Criminal Violence.* New York: Pantheon.

Danet, Brenda (1980) "Language in the Legal Process," 14(3) *Law & Society Review* 445.

Danzig, Richard (1973) "Toward the Creation of a Complementary Decentralized System of Justice," 26 *Stanford Law Review* 1.

Danzig, Richard, and Michael Lowy (1975) "Everyday Disputes and Mediation in the United States: A Reply to Professor Felstiner," 10 *Law & Society Review* 675.

Davis, Robert C. (1982) "Mediation: The Brooklyn Experiment," in Roman Tomasic and Malcolm Feeley, eds., *Neighborhood Justice: Assessment of an Emerging Idea.* New York: Longman.

Davis, Robert C., Martha Tichane, and Deborah Grayson (1980) *Mediation and Arbitration as Alternatives to Prosecution in Felony Arrest Cases: An Evaluation of the Brooklyn Dispute Resolution Center.* New York: Vera Institute of Justice.

Dear, Michael (1981) "Social and Spatial Reproduction of the Mentally Ill," in Michael Dear and Allen J. Scott, eds., *Urbanization and Urban Planning in Capitalist Society.* London: Methuen.

Dear, Michael and Allen J. Scott (1981) "Towards A Framework for Analysis," in Michael Dear and Allen J. Scott, eds., *Urbanization and Urban Planning in Capitalist Society.* London: Methuen.

DeJong, William, Gail A. Goolkasian, and Daniel McGillis (1983) *The Use of Mediation and Arbitration in Small Claims Disputes.* Washington, D.C.: U.S. Department of Justice, National Institute of Justice.

Delappa, Fred (1977) "Citizen Dispute Settlement: A New Look at An Old Method," 51(8) *Florida Bar Journal* 516.

Delappa, Fred (1983) *Resolving Disputes: An Alternative Approach: A Handbook for the Establishment of Dispute Settlement Centers.* Washington, D.C.: American Bar Association, Young Lawyers Division and the Special Committee on Alternative Means of Dispute Resolution.

D'Errico, Peter (1978) "A Critique of 'Critical Social Thought About Law' and Some Comments on Decoding Capitalist Culture." Paper presented to the Second Conference on Critical Legal Studies, Madison, Wisconsin, November 10–12, 1978.

Diamond, Stanley (1974) "The Rule of Law vs. the Order of Custom," in Richard Quinney, ed., *Criminal Justice in America: A Critical Understanding.* Boston: Little, Brown.

Dispute Resolution (1979–1986) Washington, D.C.: American Bar Association Special Committee on Resolution of Minor Disputes (quarterly).

DiTomaso, Nancy (1978) "The Expropriation of the Means of Administration: Class Struggle Over the U. S. Department of Labor," 7 *Kapitalistate* 81.

Donzelot, Jacques (1979) *The Policing of Families*. New York: Pantheon.

Doo, Leigh-Woo (1973) "Dispute Settlement in Chinese-American Communities," 21 *American Journal of Comparative Law* 627.

Downie, Leonard (1971) *Justice Denied: The Case for Reform of the Courts*. New York: Praeger.

Drier, Peter (1979) "The Case for Transitional Reform," 9(4) *Social Policy* 5.

Durkheim, Emile (1964) *The Division of Labor in Society*. New York: Free Press.

Eagleton, Terry (1976) *Criticism and Ideology: A Study in Marxist Literary Theory*. London: Verso.

Early, Bert H. (1972) "National Institute of Justice—A Proposal," 74 *West Virginia Law Review* 226.

Eaton, John (1966) *Political Economy*. New York: International Publishers.

Edel, Matthew (1981) "Prolegomena to a Theory of Urbanization and Urban Planning," in Michael Dear and Allen J. Scott, eds., *Urbanization and Urban Planning in Capitalist Society*. London: Methuen.

Educational and Psychological Development Corporation (1978) "Citizens Dispute Settlement Project, Office of the City Attorney, Minneapolis, Minnesota; First Year Evaluation, September 1976–September 1977." Columbus, Ohio: Educational and Psychological Development Corporation.

Edwards, Richard (1978) "Social Relations of Production at the Point of Production," 8 *The Insurgent Sociologist* 109.

Edwards, Richard (1979) *Contested Terrain: The Transformation of the Workplace in the Twentieth Century*. New York: Basic Books.

Ehrenreich, John (1981) "Adding Up the Unemployed," 233 *The Nation* 1 (July 25–August 1).

Esland, Geoff (1980) "Diagnosis and Therapy," in Geoff Esland and Graeme Salaman, eds., *The Politics of Work and Occupations*. Toronto: University of Toronto Press.

Feeley, Malcolm (1980) *The Process is the Punishment*. New York: Russell Sage Foundation.

Felstiner, William L. F. (1974) "Influences of Social Organization On Dispute Processing," 9 *Law & Society* Review 63.

Felstiner, William L. F., and Lynne A. Williams (1978) "Mediation as an

Alternative to Criminal Prosecution," 2(3) *Law and Human Behavior* 223.

Felstiner, William L. F., and Lynne A. Williams (1982) "Community Mediation in Dorchester, Massachusetts," in Roman Tomasic and Malcolm Feeley, eds., *Neighborhood Justice: Assessment of An Emgerging Idea*. New York: Longman.

Fine, Bob (1979a) "Struggles Against Discipline: The Theory and Politics of Michael Foucault," 9 *Capital and Class* 75.

Fine, Bob, ed. (1979b) *Capitalism and the Rule of Law*. London: Hutchison.

Fischer, E. A. (1975) "Community Courts—An Alternative to Conventional Criminal Adjudication," 24 *American University Law Review* 1253.

Fiss, Owen M. (1984) "Against Settlement," 93 *Yale Law Journal* 1073.

Florida Supreme Court, Office of the State Courts Administrator (1978) *Citizen Dispute Settlement Guideline Manual*. Tallahassee, Fla.: Office of the State Courts Administrator.

Folberg, Jay, and Alison Taylor (1984) *Mediation: A Comprehensive Guide To Resolving Conflicts Without Litigation*. San Francisco: Jossey-Bass.

Ford Foundation (1978a) *New Approaches to Conflict Resolution*. New York: Ford Foundation.

Ford Foundation (1978b) *Mediating Social Conflict*. New York: Ford Foundation.

Ford Foundation (1983) *Newsletter* (April).

Foucault, Michel (1977) *Discipline and Punish: The Birth of the Prison*. New York: Pantheon.

Fox, Ken, Mary Jo Hetzel, Tom Riddell, Nancy Rose, and Jerry Sazama (1981) "Introduction: The Nature of the Public Sector," in Economics Education Project, Union for Radical Political Economics, eds., *Crisis in the Public Sector*. New York: Monthly Review Press/Union for Radical Political Economics.

Fraser, Andrew (1978) "The Legal Theory We Need Now," 8 *Socialist Review* 147.

Freedman, Lawrence (1984) *State Legislation on Dispute Resolution*. Washington, D.C.: Special Committee on Dispute Resolution, American Bar Association.

Friedman, Andrew L. (1977) *Industry and Labour: Class Struggle at Work and Monopoly Capitalism*. London: Macmillan.

Friesen, Ernest C., Jr., Edward C. Gallas, and Nesta M. Gallas (1971) *Managing the Courts*. Indianapolis, Ind.: Bobbs-Merrill.

Fuller, Lon (1971) "Mediation—Its Forms and Functions," 44 *Southern California Law Review* 305.

Galanter, Marc (1974) "Why the Haves Come Out Ahead: Speculations on the Limits of Legal Change," 9 *Law & Society Review* 95.

Galanter, Marc (1979) *Justice in Many Rooms*. A working paper prepared for the Disputes Processing Research Program. Madison, Wisconsin: University of Wisconsin Law School.

Galanter, Marc (1983) "Reading the Landscape of Disputes: What We Think We Know and Don't Know (and Think We Know) About Our Allegedly Contentious and Litigious Society," 31(1) *UCLA Law Review* 4.

Gamson, William (1968) *Power and Discontent*. Homewood, Ill.: The Dorsey Press.

Garofalo, James and Kevin Connelly (1980a) "Dispute Resolution Centers, Part I: Major Features and Processes," *Criminal Justice Abstracts* 416 (November).

Garofalo, James, and Kevin Connelly (1980b) "Dispute Resolution Centers, Part II: Issues and Future Directions," *Criminal Justice Abstracts* 576 (December).

Garth, Bryant (1982) "The Movement Toward Procedural Informalism in North America and Western Europe: A Critical Survey," in Richard L. Abel, ed., *The Politics of Informal Justice, Volume 2: Comparative Studies*. New York: Academic Press.

Gartman, David (1978) "Marx and the Labor Process: An Interpretation," 8 *The Insurgent Sociologist* 97.

Gendrot, Sophie N. (1982) "Governmental Responses to Popular Movements: France and the United States," in Normal I. Fainstein and Susan S. Fainstein, eds., *Urban Policy under Capitalism*. Beverly Hills, Calif.: Sage Publications.

Gintis, Herbert (1980) "Communication and Politics: Marxism and the 'Problem' of Liberal Democracy," 50–51 *Socialist Review* 189.

Godelier, Maurice (1973) "Structure and Contradiction in Capital," in Robin Blackburn, ed., *Ideology in Social Science*. New York: Vintage Books.

Goffman, Erving (1961) *Asylums*. New York: Doubleday.

Gold, David A., Clarence Y. H. Lo, and Erik Olin Wright (1975) "Recent Developments in Marxist Theories of the Capitalist State," 5, 6 *Monthly Review* 29/36.

Goldberg, Stephen B., Eric Green, and Frank E. A. Sander, eds. (1985) *Dispute Resolution*. Boston: Little, Brown.

Gordon, David (1976) "Capitalist Efficiency and Socialist Efficiency," 28 *Monthly Review* 19.

Gordon, David (1977) "Capitalism and the Roots of Urban Crisis," in

Roger E. Alcaly and David Mermelstein, eds., *The Fiscal Crisis of American Cities*. New York: Vintage.

Gorz, André (1967) *Strategy for Labor*. Boston: Beacon Press.

Gorz, André (1972) "Domestic Contradictions of Advanced Capitalism," in Richard Edwards et al., eds., *The Capitalist System*. Englewood-Cliffs, N. J.: Prentice-Hall.

Gough, Ian (1972) "Marx's Theory of Productive and Unproductive Labor," 76 *New Left Review* 51.

Gramsci, Antonio (1971) *Selections from the Prison Notebooks*. New York: International Publishers.

Grau, Charles W. (1982) "Whatever Happened to Politics? A Critique of Structuralist Marxist Accounts of State and Law," in Piers Bierne and Richard Quinney, eds., *Marxism and Law*. New York: John Wiley and Sons.

Grau, Charles W., and Jane Kahn (1980) "Working the Damned, the Dumb, and the Destitute: The Politics of Community Service Restitution," in James J. Alfini, ed., *Misdemeanor Courts: Policy Concerns and Research Perspectives*. Chicago: American Judicature Society.

Greason, A. L. (1980) "Humanists as Mediators: An Experiment in the Courts of Maine," 66 *ABA Journal* 576.

Green, Mark, and Norman Waitzman (1980) "Cost, Benefit, and Class," 7 *Working Papers for a New Society* 39.

Greenberg, David (1975) "Problems in Community Corrections," 10(1) *Issues in Criminology* (Spring).

Gregory, Derek, and John Urry, eds. (1985) *Social Relations & Spatial Structures*. New York: St. Martin's Press.

Habermas, Jurgen (1975) *Legitimation Crisis*. Boston: Beacon Press.

Hall, Stuart (1982) "The Rediscovery of Ideology: Return of the Repressed in Media Studies," in Michael Gurevitch, Tony Bennett, James Curran and Janet Woollacott, eds., *Culture, Society, and the Media*. New York: Methuen.

Hall, Stuart (1983) "The Problem of Ideology: Marxism Without Guarantees," in Betty Matthews, ed., *Marx: A Hundred Years On*. London: Lawrence and Wishart.

Harrington, Christine (1980) "Voluntariness, Consent and Coercion in Adjudicating Minor Disputes: The Neighborhood Justice Center," in John Brigham and Don Brown, eds., *Policy Implementation: Choosing Between Penalties and Incentives*. Beverly Hills, Calif.: Sage Publications.

Harrington, Christine (1982) "Delegalization Reform Movements: A Historical Analysis," in Richard L. Abel, ed., *The Politics of Infor-*

mal Justice, Volume 1: The American Experience. New York: Academic Press.

Harrington, Christine (1984) "The Politics of Participation and Nonparticipation in Dispute Processes," 6(2) *Law and Policy* 203.

Harrington, Christine (1985) *Shadow Justice: The Ideology and Institutionalization of Alternatives to Courts.* Westport, Conn.: Greenwood Press.

Harvey, David (1976) "Labor, Capital, and Class Struggle Around the Built Environment in Advanced Capitalist Societies," 6 *Politics and Society* 265.

Harvey, David (1981) "The Urban Process Under Capitalism," in Michael Dear and Allen J. Scott, eds., *Urbanization and Urban Planning in Capitalist Society.* London: Methuen.

Hay, Douglas, Peter Linebaugh, John G. Rule, E. P. Thompson, and Cal Winslow (1975) *Albion's Fatal Tree: Crime and Society in Eighteenth-Century England.* New York: Pantheon.

Heilbroner, Robert (1976) "The American Plan," *The New York Times Magazine* 9 (January 25).

Heilbroner, Robert (1978) *Beyond Boom and Crash.* New York: W. W. Norton.

Henry, Stuart (1982) "Factory Law: The Changing Disciplinary Technology of Industrial Social Control," 10(4) *International Journal of the Sociology of Law* 365.

Henry, Stuart (1983) *Private Justice: Towards Integrated Theorizing in the Sociology of Law.* London: Routledge and Kegan Paul.

Herbers, John (1979) "Labor-Style Negotiations Tested to Coordinate City Plans in U. S.," *New York Times* 1 (November 25).

Heydebrand, Wolf (1977) "Organizational Contradictions in Public Bureaucracies: Toward a Marxian Theory of Organizations," 18 *Sociological Quarterly* 83.

Heydebrand, Wolf (1978) "The Context of Public Bureaucracies: An Organizational Analysis of Federal District Courts," 11 *Law & Society Review* 759.

Heydebrand, Wolf (1979) "The Technocratic Administration of Justice," in Steven Spitzer, ed., *Research in Law and Sociology*, Volume 2. Greenwich, Conn.: JAI Press.

Heydebrand, Wolf, and Carol Seron (1981) "The Double Bind of the Capitalist Judicial System," 9 *International Journal of the Sociology of Law* 407.

Hill, Richard Child (1976) "Fiscal Crisis and Political Struggle in the Decaying Central City," 4/5 *Kapitalistate* 31.

Hirsch, Joachim (1978) "The State Apparatus and Social Reproduction: Elements of a Theory of the Bourgeois State," in John Holloway

174   Bibliography

and Sol Picciotto, eds., *State and Capital: A Marxist Debate*. Austin: University of Texas Press.

Hirsch, Joachim (1981) "The Apparatus of the State, the Reproduction of Capital," in Michael Dear and Allen J. Scott, eds., *Urbanization and Urban Planning in Capitalist Society*. London: Methuen.

Hirsch, Joachim (1983) "The Fordist Security State and New Social Movements," 10/11 *Kapitalistate* 75.

Hirschhorn, Larry (1978) "The Political Economy of Social Service Rationalization: A Developmental View," 2 *Contemporary Crises* 63.

Hofstadter, Richard (1955) *The Age of Reform*. New York: Vintage.

Holloway, John, and Sol Picciotto (1978) "Introduction: Towards a Materialist Theory of the State," in John Holloway and Sol Picciotto, eds., *State and Capital: A Marxist Debate*. Austin: University of Texas Press.

Horwitz, Morton (1977) *The Transformation of American Law: 1780–1860*. Cambridge, Mass.: Harvard University Press.

Humphries, Drew, and David F. Greenberg (1981) "Social Control and Social Formation: Marxian Analysis," in Donald Black, ed., *Toward A General Theory of Social Control*. New York: Academic Press.

Hunt, Alan (1977) "Theory and Politics in the Identification of the Working Class," in Alan Hunt, ed., *Class and Class Structure*. London: Lawrence and Wishart.

Hunt, Alan (1981) "Dichotomy and Contradiction in the Sociology of Law," in Piers Bierne and Richard Quinney, eds., *Marxism and Law*. New York: John Wiley.

Hylton, John (1981) "The Growth of Punishment: Imprisonment and Community Corrections in Canada," 15 *Crime and Social Justice* 18.

Hyman, Richard (1980) "Trade Unions, Control, and Resistance," in Geoff Esland and Graeme Salaman, eds., *The Politics of Work and Occupations*. Toronto: University of Toronto Press.

Hymer, Stephen (1978) "International Politics/International Economics," 29 *Monthly Review* 15.

Ignatieff, Michael (1978) *A Just Measure of Pain: The Penitentiary in the Industrial Revolution, 1750–1850*. New York: Pantheon.

Institute for Labor Education and Research (1982) *What's Wrong with the U. S. Economy?* Boston: South End Press.

Issacman, Barbara, and Allen Issacman (1982) "A Socialist Legal System in the Making: Mozambique Before and After Independence," in Richard Abel, ed., *The Politics of Informal Justice: Comparative Studies*, Volume 2. New York: Academic Press.

Jankovic, Ivan (1977) "Labor Market and Imprisonment," 8 *Crime and Social Justice* 17.

Jessop, Bob (1980) "On Recent Marxist Theories of Law, the State, and Juridico-Political Ideology," 8 *International Journal of the Sociology of Law* 339.

Jessop, Bob (1983) *The Capitalist State.* New York: New York University Press.

Johnson, Earl (1978) "Courts and the Community," in *State Courts: A Blueprint for the Future.* Denver, Colo.: National Center for State Courts.

Johnson, Earl, Valerie Kantor, and Elizabeth Schwartz (1977) *Outside the Courts: A Survey of Diversion Alternatives in Civil Cases.* Denver, Colo.: National Center for State Courts.

Johnston, Paul (1981) "Public Sector Unionism," in Economics Education Project, Union for Radical Political Economics, eds., *Crisis in the Public Sector.* New York: Monthly Review Press/Union for Radical Political Economics.

Katz, Jack (1984) *Poor People's Lawyers in Transition.* New Brunswick, N. J.: Rutgers University Press.

Katz, M. B. (1978) "Origins of the Institutional State," 1(4) *Marxist Perspectives* 6–22 (Winter).

Katznelson, Ira (1981) *City Trenches: Urban Politics and the Patterning of Class in the United States.* New York: Pantheon.

Kidder, Robert L. (1980) "Down to Earth Justice: Pitfalls on the Road to Legal Decentralization," in Melvin J. Lerner and Sally C. Lerner, eds., *The Justice Motive in Social Behavior.* New York: Plenum Press.

Kidder, Robert L. (1981) "The End of the Road? Problems in the Analysis of Disputes," 15(34) *Law & Society Review* 717.

Kinsey, Richard (1978) "Marxism and the Law," 5(2) *British Journal of Law and Society* 202.

Kittrie, Nicholas (1971) *The Right to be Different.* Baltimore, Md.: Penguin.

Klare, Karl (1982) "Labor Law and the Liberal Political Imagination," 62 *Socialist Review* 45 (March-April).

Klein, James H., Jane Ratcliffe, Joseph Griesta, and Clement Risk (1978) *Neighborhood Justice in Chicago: A City of Neighborhoods.* A report of the Neighborhood Justice Task Force prepared for the Chicago Bar Association. Chicago: Chicago Bar Association.

Kotler, Milton (1969) *Neighborhood Government: The Local Foundations of Political Life.* Indianapolis, Ind.: Bobbs-Merrill.

Laclau, Ernesto (1983) " 'Socialism,' the 'People,' 'Democracy': The Transformation of Hegemonic Logic" 7 *Social Text* 115.

Laclau, Ernesto, and Chantal Mouffe (Interview with) (1982) "Recasting Marxism: Hegemony and New Political Movements," 12(6) *Socialist Review* 91.

Lasch, Christopher (1981) "The Crisis of Confidence," 1(1) *Democracy* 25.

Lazerson, Mark H. (1982) "In the Halls of Justice, the Only Justice Is in the Halls," in Richard L. Abel, ed., *The Politics of Informal Justice, Volume 1: The American Experience.* New York: Academic Press.

Lefcourt, Carol (1984) "Women, Mediation, and Family Law," *Clearinghouse Review* 266 (July).

Lefebvre, Henri (1976) *The Survival of Capitalism.* London: Allison and Busby.

Leontief, Wassily (1982) "What Hope for the Economy," *New York Review of Books* 31 (April 12).

Lerner, Max (1957) "The Supreme Court and Industrial Society," in Robert G. McCloskey, ed., *The Supreme Court and Industrial Society.* New York: Vintage.

Linebaugh, Peter (1976) "Karl Marx, the Theft of Wood, and Working Class Composition: A Contribution to the Current Debate," 6 *Crime and Social Justice* 5.

Lively, Martin (1977) *Memorandum to Proposed Neighborhood Justice Center Grantees, Grant Application Guidelines and Procedures.* Washington, D.C.: Training and Testing Division, Office of Technology Transfer, Law Enforcement Assistance Administration.

Lovins, Amory B. (1977) *Soft-Energy Paths.* San Francisco: Friends of the Earth International.

Magaziner, Ira, and Robert Reich (1982) *Minding America's Business: The Decline and Rise of the American Economy.* New York: Harcourt Brace Jovanovich.

Markham, Wayne (1979) "Close Encounters of the Condo Kind," *Miami Herald* (October 21).

Marks, Jonathan B., Earl Johnson Jr., and Peter Szanton (1984) *Dispute Resolution in America: Processes In Evolution.* Washington, D.C.: National Institute for Dispute Resolution.

Martinson, Pati L. (1981) *The Manual: A "How To" Guide for the Management and Development of Mediation Projects Designed for Non-Profit and Government Agencies.* Denver, Colo.: Denver Commission on Community Relations.

Marx, Karl [1867] (1967) *Capital,* Volume 1. New York: International Publishers.

Marx, Karl (1970a) *The German Ideology.* New York: International Publishers.

Marx, Karl [1859] (1970b) *A Contribution to the Critique of Political Economy.* New York: International Publishers.

Maslow, Abraham (1970) *Motivation and Personality.* New York: Harper and Row.

Mather, Lynn, and Barbara Yngvesson (1981) "Language, Audience, and the Transformation of Disputes," 15 *Law & Society Review* 775.

Mathiesen, Thomas (1980) *Law, Society, and Political Action: Towards A Strategy Under Late Capitalism*. New York: Academic Press.

McEwen, Craig, and Richard J. Maiman (1981) "Small Claims Mediation in Maine: An Empirical Assessment," 33 *Maine Law Review* 237.

McEwen, Craig, and Richard J. Maiman (1984) "Mediation In Small Claims Court: Achieving Compliance Through Consent," 18(1) *Law & Society Review* 11.

McGillis, Daniel (1980a) *Dispute Processing Projects: A Preliminary Directory*. Cambridge, Mass.: Harvard Center for Criminal Justice.

McGillis, Daniel (1980b) "Recent Developments in Minor Dispute Processing," 5 *Dispute Resolution* 12 (Washington, D.C.: ABA Special Committee on Resolution of Minor Disputes).

McGillis, Daniel (1982) "Minor Dispute Processing: A Review of Recent Developments," in Roman Tomasic and Malcolm Feeley, eds., *Neighborhood Justice: Assessment of an Emerging Idea*. New York: Longman.

McGillis, Daniel, and Joan Mullen (1977) *Neighborhood Justice Centers: An Analysis of Potential Models*. Washington, D.C.: U. S. Government Printing Office.

McLauchlan, Gregory (1975) "LEAA: A Case Study in the Development of the Social Industrial Complex," 4 *Crime and Social Justice* 15.

Melossi, Dario (1979) "Institutions of Social Control and Capitalist Organization of Work," in Bob Fine, ed., *Capitalism and the Rule of Law*. London: Hutchinson.

Merry, Sally E. (1979) "Going to Court: Strategies of Dispute Management in an American Urban Neighborhood," 13 *Law & Society Review* 891.

Merry, Sally E. (1982a) "Defining Success in the Neighborhood Justice Movement," in Roman Tomasic and Malcolm Feeley, eds., *Neighborhood Justice: Assessment of an Emerging Idea*. New York: Longman.

Merry, Sally E. (1982b) "The Social Organization of Mediation in Non-Industrial Societies: Implications for Informal Community Justice in America," in Richard L. Abel, ed., *The Politics of Informal Justice, Volume 2: Comparative Studies*. New York: Academic Press.

Merry, Sally, and Susan Silbey (1984) "What do Plaintiffs Want? Reexamining the Concept of Dispute," 9/2 *The Justice System Journal* 151.

Miliband, Ralph (1973) *The State in Capitalist Society*. London: Quarter Books.

Milovanovic, Dragan (1981) "The Commodity Exchange Theory of Law: In Search of a Perspective," 16 *Crime and Social Justice* 41.

Moberg, David (1980) "Work and American Culture: The Ideal of Self-Determination and the Prospects for Socialism," 50–51 *Socialist Review* 19.

Mollenkopf, John (1977) "The Crisis of the Public Sector in America's Cities," in Roger E. Alcaly and David Mermelstein, eds., *The Fiscal Crisis of American Cities*. New York: Vintage.

Mollenkopf, John (1981) "Neighborhood Political Development and the Politics of Urban Growth: Boston and San Francisco 1958–78," 5(1) *International Journal of Urban and Regional Research* 15.

Morgan, Patricia (1981) "From Battered Wife to Program Client: The State's Shaping of Social Problems," 9 *Kapitalistate* 17.

Moriarity, William F., Jr., Thomas L. Norris, and Luis Salus (1977) *Dade County Citizen Dispute Settlement Program: Evaluation*. Miami, Fla.: Dade County Criminal Justice Planning Unit.

Morris, David (1982) *Self-Reliant Cities: Energy and the Transformation of Urban America*. San Francisco: Sierra Club Books.

Morris, David, and Karl Hess (1975) *Neighborhood Power: Returning Political and Economic Power to Community Life*. Boston: Beacon Press.

Mouffe, Chantal (1979) "Hegemony and Ideology in Gramsci," in Chantal Mouffe, ed., *Gramsci and Marxist Theory*. London: Routledge and Kegan Paul.

Nader, Laura, ed. (1980) *No Access to Law: Alternatives to the American Judicial System*. New York: Academic Press.

Nader, Laura (1984) "The Recurrent Dialectic Between Legality and Its Alternatives: The Limitations of Binary Thinking. Jerold S. Auerbach, Justice Without Law," 132(3) *University of Pennsylvania Law Review* 621.

Nader, Laura, and Linda Singer (1976) "Law in the Future: What are the Choices?" 51 *California State Bar Journal* 281.

National Center for State Courts (1978) *Planning in State Courts: Trends and Developments, 1976–78*. Williamsburg, Va.: National Center for State Courts.

Neighborhood Justice Center of Atlanta (1986) *Program Beneficiary Statistics*.

Neighborhood Justice Center of Houston (1986) "Dispute Resolution Centers: A Comprehensive Approach to Resolving Citizen Disputes."

Neighborhood Justice Center, Houston, Texas (1980) *Brochure*.

Neighborhood Justice Center of Los Angeles (1985) *Project Summary* (September).

Neubeck, Kenneth J. (1977) "Capitalism as Therapy?" 8(1) *Social Policy* 41.

Neumann, Franz (1957) "The Change in the Function of Law in Modern Society," in F. Neumann, *The Democratic and the Authoritarian State.* New York: Free Press.

Newfield, Jack, and Paul Dubrul (1977) *The Abuse of Power.* New York: Penguin Books.

Nichols, Theodore (1980) "Management, Ideology, and Practice," in Geoff Esland and Graeme Salaman, eds., *The Politics of Work and Occupations.* Toronto: University of Toronto Press.

Nicolau, George (1975) *Community Mediator Training Manual.* New York: Institute for Mediation and Conflict Resolution.

NIDR, National Institute for Dispute Resolution (1981) Untitled planning document (May).

NIDR, National Institute for Dispute Resolution (1984) *Forum* (June).

NIDR, National Institute for Dispute Resolution (1986) *Forum* (April).

Noble, David F. (1978) "Social Choice in Machine Design: The Case of Automatically Controlled Machine Tools, and a Challenge for Labor," 8 *Politics and Society* 313.

North Carolina Bar Association (1985) *Dispute Resolution.* A Task Force Report. Raleigh, North Carolina.

O'Connor, James (1973) *The Fiscal Crisis of the State.* New York: St. Martin's Press.

O'Connor, James (1978) "The Democratic Movement in the United States," 7 *Kapitalistate* 15.

O'Connor, James (1981a) "Accumulation Crisis: The Problem and Its Setting," 5 *Contemporary Crises* 109.

O'Connor, James (1981b) "The Meaning of Crisis," *International Journal of Urban and Regional Research* 301.

O'Connor, James (1984) *Accumulation Crisis.* New York: Basil Blackwell.

Offe, Claus (1975) "The Theory of the Capitalist State and the Problem of Policy Formation," in Leon Lindberg et al., eds., *Stress and Contradiction in Modern Capitalism.* Lexington, Mass.: D.C. Heath and Co.

Offe, Claus (1984) *Contradictions of the Welfare State.* Edited by John Keane. Cambridge, Mass.: M.I.T. Press.

Parsons, Talcot (1949) *The Structure of Social Action.* New York: Free Press.

Pashukanis, Evgeny B. (1978) *Law and Marxism: A General Theory.* Edited by Chris Arthur. London: Ink Links.

Pearson, J., and N. Thoennes (1982) "Divorce Mediation: Strengths and Weaknesses Over Time," in H. Davidson, Larry Ray, and R. Horowitz, eds., *Alternative Means of Family Dispute Resolution*. Washington, D.C.: American Bar Association.

Perlman, Janice E. (1978) "Grassroots Participation From Neighborhood to Nation," in Stuart Langton, ed., *Citizen Participation in America*. Lexington, Mass.: Lexington Books.

Pignon, Dominique, and Jean Querzola (1978) "Dictatorship and Democracy in Production," in André Gorz, ed., *The Division of Labour: The Labour Process and Class Struggle in Modern Capitalism*. Sussex, England: The Harvester Press.

Pinellas County Citizen Dispute Settlement Project (1978) *Final Report*. St. Petersburg, Florida.

Piven, Frances Fox (1972) "The New Urban Programs: The Strategy of Federal Intervention," in Richard A. Cloward and Frances Fox Piven, eds., *The Politics of Turmoil: Poverty, Race, and the Urban Crisis*. New York: Vintage.

Piven, Frances Fox, and Richard Cloward (1971) *Regulating the Poor*. New York: Vintage.

Piven, Frances Fox and Richard A. Cloward (1972) "Black Control of Cities: Heading It Off by Metropolitan Government," in Richard A. Cloward and Frances Fox Piven, eds., *The Politics of Turmoil: Poverty, Race, and the Urban Crisis*. New York: Vintage.

Piven, Frances Fox, and Richard Cloward (1979) *Poor People's Movements*. New York: Vintage.

Piven, Frances Fox, and Richard A. Cloward (1982) *The New Class War: Reagan's Attack on the Welfare State and Its Consequences*. New York: Pantheon.

Platt, Anthony (1969) *The Child Savers: The Invention of Delinquency*. Chicago: University of Chicago Press.

Poulantzas, Nicos (1968) *Political Power and Social Classes*. London: Verso.

Poulantzas, Nicos (1978) *State, Power, Socialism*. London: Verso.

Pound, Roscoe (1940) *Organization of Courts*. Boston: Little, Brown.

Quinney, Richard (1977) *Class, State, and Crime*. New York: David McKay.

Raskin, A. H. (1982) "The Cooperative Economy," *New York Times*, Section 3, p. 1 (February 14).

Ray, Larry, and Anna L. Clarke (1985) "The Multi-Door Courthouse of the Future . . . Today" 1/1 *Ohio State Journal on Dispute Resolution*.

Ray, Larry, Prue Kestner, John R. Thweatt, Margot Leffler, Jody Le Perkins, Joseph O'Hara, and Anne Clare (1986) *Dispute Resolution Program Directory*. Washington, D.C.: Special Committee on Dispute Resolution, American Bar Association.

Reich, Robert (1982) "Industrial Policy," *The New Republic* 28 (March 31).

Reifner, Udo (1982) "Individualistic and Collective Legalization: Theory and Practice of Legal Advice for Workers in Prefascist Germany," in Richard L. Abel, ed., *The Politics of Informal Justice, Volume 2: Comparative Studies.* New York: Academic Press.

Resnick, Bill (1981) "The Right's Prospects: Can It Reconstruct America," 56 *Socialist Review* 9.

Rheinstein, Max, ed. (1954) *Max Weber on Law in Economy and Society.* Cambridge, Mass.: Harvard University Press.

Riskin, Leonard (1982) "Mediation and Lawyers," 43(1) *Ohio State Law Journal* 29.

Rodberg, Leonard, and Gelvin Stevenson (1977) "The Health Care Industry in Advanced Capitalism," 9 *The Review of Radical Political Economics* 104.

Roehl, Janice, and Royer F. Cook (1982) "The Neighborhood Justice Centers Field Test," in Roman Tomasic and Malcolm Feeley, eds., *Neighborhood Justice: Assessment of an Emerging Idea.* New York: Longman.

Rohatyn, Felix (1981) "Reconstructing America," *New York Review of Books* 16 (March 5).

Rosenberg, Morris (1972) "Let's Everybody Litigate," 50 *Texas Law Review* 1349.

Rothman, David J. (1971) *The Discovery of the Asylum: Social Order and Disorder in the New Republic.* Boston: Little, Brown.

Rubinstein, Leonard (1976) "Procedural Due Process and the Limits of the Adversary System," 11 *Harvard Civil Liberties—Civil Rights Law Review* 48.

Sale, Kirkpatrick (1980) *Human Scale.* New York: Coward, McCann and Geohagen.

Sander, Frank (1976) "Varieties of Dispute Processing," 70 *Federal Rules Decisions* 79.

Sander, Frank (1977) *Report on the National Conference on Minor Dispute Resolution.* Chicago: American Bar Association.

Santos, Boaventura de Sousa (1977) "The Law of the Oppressed: The Construction and Reproduction of Legality in Pasargada," 12 *Law & Society Review* 3.

Santos, Boaventura de Sousa (1982) "Law and Community: The Changing Nature of State Power in Late Capitalism," in Richard L. Abel, ed., *The Politics of Informal Justice, Volume 1: The American Experience.* New York: Academic Press.

Sarat, Austin, and Joel Grossman (1975) "Courts and Conflict Resolution," 60 *American Political Science Review* 1200.

Schumacher, E. F. (1973) *Small is Beautiful.* New York: Harper and Row.

Schwendiger, Herman, and Julia R. Schwendiger (1976) "Delinquency and the Collective Varieties of Youth," 5 *Crime and Social Justice* 7.

Scull, Andrew T. (1977) *Decarceration: Community Treatment and the Deviant—A Radical View.* Englewood Cliffs, N. J.: Prentice-Hall.

Sennett, Richard (1979) "The Boss's New Clothes," *New York Review of Books* 42 (February 22).

Shaiken, Harley (1979) "The Brave New World of Work in Auto," *In These Times* 12 (September 19).

Sheppard, David I., Janice Roehl, and Royer Cook (1979) *Neighborhood Justice Centers Field Test: An Interim Report.* Washington, D.C.: National Institute of Law Enforcement and Criminal Justice, Law Enforcement Assistance Administration.

Shonholtz, Raymond (1977) *Review of Alternative Dispute Mechanisms and a Government Proposal for Neighborhood Justice Centers.* San Francisco: San Francisco Community Board Program.

Shonholtz, Raymond (1984) "Neighborhood Justice Systems: Work, Structure, and Guiding Principles," 5 *Mediation Quarterly* 3.

Silbey, Susan S., and Sally E. Merry (1983) "The Problems Shape the Process: Managing Disputes in Mediation and Court." Paper presented at the 1982 meeting of the Law and Society Association, Toronto, Canada.

Silver, Allan (1974) "The Demand for Order in Civil Society: A Review of Some Themes in the History of Urban Crime, Police, and Riot," in Richard Quinney, ed., *Criminal Justice in America: A Critical Understanding.* Boston: Little, Brown.

Singer, Linda (1979) "Nonjudicial Dispute Resolution Mechanisms: The Effects on Justice for the Poor," *Clearinghouse Review* 569.

Sklar, Holly (1980) *Trilateralism.* Boston: South End Press.

Snyder, Frederick E. (1978) "Crime and Community Mediation—The Boston Experience: A Preliminary Report on the Dorchester Urban Court Program," *Wisconsin Law Review* 737.

Snyder, Frederick E. (1979) "Legal Implications of Mediation," 3(3) *Perspective* 15.

Special Task Force to the Secretary of Health, Education, and Welfare (1972) *Work in America.* Washington, D.C.: U. S. Government Printing Office.

Spence, Jack (1982) "Institutionalizing Neighborhood Courts: Two Chilean Experiences," in Richard L. Abel, ed., *The Politics of Informal Justice, Volume 2: Comparative Studies.* New York: Academic Press.

Spitzer, Steven (1979a) "Toward a Marxian Theory of Deviance," 22 *Social Problems* 638.

Spitzer, Steven (1979b) "The Rationalization of Crime Control in Capitalist Society," 3 *Contemporary Crises* 187.

Spitzer, Steven (1981) "The Political Economy of Policing," in David F. Greenberg, ed., *Crime and Capitalism.* Palo Alto, Calif.: Mayfield.

Spitzer, Steven (1982) "The Dialectics of Formal and Informal Control," in Richard L. Abel, ed., *The Politics of Informal Justice, Volume 1: The American Experience.* New York: Academic Press.

Spitzer, Steven, and Andrew Scull (1977) "Privatization and Capitalist Development: The Case of the Private Police," 25(1) *Social Programs* 18.

Starr, June (1981) "Mediation: Anthropological Perspectives," *American Legal Studies Association Forum.*

Stone, Katherine Van Wezel (1981) "The Post-War Paradigm in American Labor Law," 90(7) *Yale Law Journal* 1509.

Sudnow, David (1965) "Normal Crimes: Sociological Features of the Penal Code in a Public Defender Office," 13 *Social Problems* 255.

Sumner, Colin (1979) *Reading Ideologies: An Investigation into the Marxist Theory of Ideology and Law.* New York: Academic Press.

Szasz, Thomas (1965) *Psychiatric Justice.* New York: Macmillan.

Therborn, Goran (1980) *The Ideology of Power and the Power of Ideology.* London: Verso.

Thompson, E. P. (1966) *The Making of the English Working Class.* New York: Vintage.

Thompson, E. P. (1975) *Whigs and Hunters.* New York: Pantheon Books.

Thurow, Lester C. (1980) *The Zero-Sum Society.* New York: Penguin Books.

Tigar, Michael, and Madeleine Levy (1977) *Law and the Rise of Capitalism.* New York: Monthly Review Press.

Tolchin, Martin (1985) "Mediated Justice Being Put to Test," *New York Times* (July 21).

Tomasic, Roman (1982) "Mediation as an Alternative to Adjudication: Rhetoric and Reality in the Neighborhood Justice Movement," in Roman Tomasic and Malcolm Feeley, eds., *Neighborhood Justice: Assessment of an Emerging Idea.* New York: Longman.

Trubek, David (1979) *Understanding Courts in Context: A Preliminary Report on the Expected Contribution of the Civil Litigation Research Project to Civil Justice Research and Planning.* Submitted to the Office for

Improvements in the Administration of Justice. Washington, D.C.: U. S. Department of Justice.

Trubek, David M., and Marc Galanter (1974) "Scholars in Self-Estrangement: Some Reflections on the Crisis in Law and Development Studies in the United States," *Wisconsin Law Review* 1062.

Trzyna, Peter, and Karen Knab (1978) *Alternatives to Litigation and Adjudication: Program Designers' Guide*. Madison: Office of Planning and Research, Wisconsin Supreme Court.

Turkel, Gerald (1981) "Rational Law and Boundary Maintenance: Legitimating the 1971 Lockheed Labor Guarantee," 15(1) *Law & Society Review* 41.

Unger, Roberto (1975) *Law in Modern Society*. New York: Free Press.

United States Department of Justice, Law Enforcement Assistance Administration/ACTION (1980) *Urban Crime Prevention Program: Guideline Manual*. Washington, D.C.: United States Department of Justice.

United States House of Representatives (1978) Committee on the Judiciary. Subcommittee on Courts, Civil Liberties, and the Administration of Justice. "Dispute Resolution Act." *Hearings*. 95th Congress, 2nd Session, July 27 and August 2. Washington, D.C.: U. S. Government Printing Office.

United States House of Representatives (1979) Committee on the Judiciary. Subcommittee on Courts, Civil Liberties, and the Administration of Justice and Committee on Interstate and Foreign Commerce. Subcommittee on Consumer Protection and Finance. "Resolution of Minor Disputes." *Joint Hearings*. 96th Congress, 1st Session, June 6, 7, 14, and 18. Washington, D.C.: U. S. Government Printing Office.

Vera Institute of Justice (1977) *Felony Arrests: Their Prosecution and Disposition in New York City's Courts*. New York: The Vera Institute of Justice.

Wahrhaftig, Paul (1978) "Citizen Dispute Resolution: Whose Property?" in *Citizen Dispute Resolution Organizer's Handbook*. Pittsburgh: American Friends Service Committee.

Wahrhaftig, Paul (1982) "An Overview of Community-Oriented Citizen Dispute Resolution Programs in the United States," in Richard L. Abel, ed., *The Politics of Informal Justice, Volume 1: The American Experience*. New York: Academic Press.

Wehr, Paul (1986) "Conflict Resolution Studies: What Do We Know?" *Forum*. National Institute for Dispute Resolution (April).

Weinstein, James (1968) *The Corporate Ideal in the Liberal State*. Boston: Beacon Press.

Williams, Raymond (1977) *Marxism and Literature*. London: Oxford University Press.

Williams, Raymond (1981) *Culture*. Glasgow, Scotland: Fontana.

Willis, Paul (1977) *Learning to Labour: How Working Class Kids Get Working Class Jobs*. Princeton, N. J.: Princeton University Press.

Wilmington, Delaware Citizen Dispute Settlement Center (1979) *Brochure*.

Wolfe, Alan (1977) *The Limits of Legitimacy: Political Contradictions of American Captialism*. New York: Free Press.

Wright, Erik Olin (1975) "Alternative Perspectives in the Marxist Theory of Accumulation and Crisis," 6 *Insurgent Sociologist* 5.

Wright, Erik Olin (1978) *Class, Crisis, and the State*. New York: Schocken Books.

Zwerdling, Daniel (1980) *Workplace Democracy*. New York: Harper Colophon Books.

Index

Abel, Richard, xxxii n.1, 96, 112, 118, 132
Accommodation, 116-17, 134-35, 138-39, 140
Advocacy, 135, 156
Agnew, J. A., 71
Albany Dispute Mediation Project, 114
Alper, Benedict S., 98
Althusser, Louis, 37
American Arbitration Association, 50, 93, 97
American Bar Association, x
Arbitration, xv, 51-52, 63
Aronowitz, Stanley, 43

Baldwin, P., 139
Behavior: change in, 99, 132, 148, 149; informal dispute resolution controlling, 143, 147-48, 149-50; state control of, 57, 81, 147
Bowles, Samuel, and Herbert Gintis, 50
Braverman, Harry, 133
Brooklyn Dispute Mediation Center, 106, 130
Burawoy, Michael, 75, 82

Cain, Maureen, xxvii, 160
Capital: xxix, 5, 6, 29, 37, 43; consolidation of, 155; ideology and, 131; and judicial system, 51; logic of, 26, 44; prerogatives of, 51, 56, 72; social formation of, 26. *See also* Capitalism
Capital accumulation: xiv, 33, 43, 58; conditions for, 28, 51; coordination of, 49; rate of, 53. *See also* Capital expansion
Capital expansion, 4, 5, 6, 11, 15, 44, 49, 50, 52, 55, 72, 154, 155. *See also* Capital accumulation
Capitalism, xiv, 3, 4, 6, 33, 145; class struggle and, 4; contradictions, 4-6, 10, 16, 42, 67; and NDR, xiv; requirements for expansion, 55; social relations of, 88. *See also* Crisis
Capitalist rationality, 42, 67
Capitalist state. *See* State
Centralization of authority, 94-95
Citizen Utility Boards, 151
Class conflict. *See* Conflict, class
Class struggle, 3-10, 13, 14, 25-27, 35, 44, 83; in communities, 21; *See also* Conflict, class

About the Author

RICHARD HOFRICHTER is a legal sociologist and social critic residing in Washington, D.C. He has contributed chapters to *The Politics of Informal Justice*, *Neighborhood Justice*, and *Victims, Offenders, and Alternative Sanctions*.